SEEING KRISHNA

SEEING KRISHNA

THE RELIGIOUS WORLD OF A BRAHMAN FAMILY IN VRINDABAN

Margaret H. Case

OXFORD
UNIVERSITY PRESS

2000

OXFORD
UNIVERSITY PRESS

Oxford New York
Athens Auckland Bangkok Bogotá Buenos Aires Calcutta
Cape Town Chennai Dar es Salaam Delhi Florence Hong Kong Istanbul
Karachi Kuala Lumpur Madrid Melbourne Mexico City Mumbai
Nairobi Paris São Paulo Singapore Taipei Tokyo Toronto Warsaw

and associated companies in
Berlin Ibadan

Published by Oxford University Press, Inc.
198 Madison Avenue, New York, New York 110016

Oxford is a registered trademark of Oxford University Press

Library of Congress Cataloging-in-Publication Data
Case, Margret H.
Seeing Krishna / the religious world of a Brahman family in
Vrindaban / Margaret H. Case.
p. cm.
Includes bibliographical references and index.
ISBN 0-19-513010-3; 0-19-513011-1 (pbk.)
1. Religious life—Chaitanya (Sect) 2. Puruṣottama Gosvāmī,
Maharaj. 3. Goswami, Shrivatsa. 4. Vrindāvan (India)—Religious
life and customs. I. Title.
BL1285,392. P87C37 2000
294,5'512'09542—dc21 9B53863

1 3 5 7 9 8 6 4 2

Printed in the United States of America
on acid-free paper

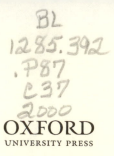

For my mother, Mary A. Harrison,
and Margaret M. Flinsch,
and in memory of
Nancy Pearson,
with love and gratitude

PROLOGUE

In November 1992, the god Krishna appeared to a group of devotees in the town of Vrindaban in north India. He manifested in the form of a large black bee or beetle, and he appeared three times; his image was irrefutably captured on videotape. I was present at all three appearances; when I tell the story, people often ask, "Do you believe it was really Krishna?" My answer has come to be, "It all depends. In the context, yes." And context is everything.[1] Context is the story of this book.

I first came to Jaisingh Ghera, the home in Vrindaban of the Goswami family, as a friend of the family. Although I had visited India in the late 1950s, right out of college, and had gone on to study Indian history as a graduate student at the University of Chicago, I made my career as an editor at Princeton University Press and, to my regret, did not return to India. As editor of a book for which Shrivatsa Goswami was a collaborator, I met him about 1980. I visited Vrindaban for a few hours during a quick trip to India later that year; Shrivatsa and his wife stayed at our house in New Jersey one weekend soon thereafter. In 1990, our acquaintance was renewed, and he invited me to come to Vrindaban; thanks to a generous leave granted by Princeton University Press, I was able to do so the next year—and then returned frequently.

Shrivatsa is the elder son of Mahārāj jī, the central figure in this account; Mahārāj jī is a leading priest in the traditional Caitanyaite Vaiṣṇava lineage serving Rādhāramaṇa temple in Vrindaban. I lived in the Goswamis' ashram (family compound) a few months a year for the next several years, experiencing the life there before I began to think about writing about this book. Throughout my stays, I was included in family events and the celebrations of the extended family of devotees. As I traveled back and forth between my family in New Jersey and my "second home" in Vrindaban, my perspective also changed back and forth. This is reflected in the narration of this story.

ACKNOWLEDGMENTS

My greatest debt is to Shrivatsa Goswami, and this is his book as much as mine. His ability to communicate a deep knowledge and understanding of Caitanyaite Vaiṣṇavism, his openness and hospitality to Western scholars, and his warm friendship and guidance have been enjoyed by several scholarly generations. I have had the privilege and pleasure of sitting with him for many discussions and have always learned from his explanations of the events that constitute the life of the ashram. His informal discourses are the primary source for this book, and his voice will often be heard in these pages. Because the book reflects what I have learned, however, not what he understands, my name and not his is on the title page.

Shrivatsa's father, Jagadguru Puruṣottama Gosvāmī Mahārāja (Mahārāj jī), a man of great religious experience and learning in the Vaiṣṇava texts, is the central human focus of the ashram, although Shrivatsa and his brother, Veṇu Gopāla, are taking on more of the responsibilities as time goes on. Mahārāj jī is the human protagonist of this book. When the manuscript was finished and I showed him a copy for his blessing, he said, "But you know nothing about me!"—which is true. And yet, to the extent that he can be known by what he says and does, by what he has created and how, I have drawn his portrait. For opening his home and allowing me to share in his extended family's life, I am grateful.

The other members of the Goswami family living in Jaisingh Ghera—Shrivatsa's wife, Sandhyā; his sons, known to me by their family names of Rājū and Sonī; his late mother, "Mātā jī"; and his brother, Veṇu

Gopāla—have all offered friendship, hospitality, and care. The staff of Jaisingh Ghera have always offered their services with humor and affection. I want especially to thank Jagdish Prakash, general manager of Jaisingh Ghera, who has been cheerfully helpful on many occasions.

The long-term foreign residents of the ashram, Robyn Beeche, Michael Duffy, and the late Asimakrishna Dasa, have been friends and colleagues from the beginning. Each of them has devoted abundant talents and energies to the work of the ashram and has served as well to make the lives of foreign visitors enjoyable and rewarding. With Robyn, especially, I have shared discovery, information, and understanding over the years. She has guided me through many pitfalls (and picked me up after pratfalls), encouraged, fed, and humored me, and worked with me on innumerable joint undertakings. We have shared some extraordinary experiences, and I thank her. Many of her photographs adorn this book.

A wider "extended family" of nonresident family and close devotees participate in the life-cycle rituals of the Goswami family and in the activities of the ritual calendar. This wider circle of family and friends have shared their experiences, included me in their activities, and involved me in ways that were limited only by my own reserve. I particularly want to thank Sashi Kumar, Chulbul Modi, Veena Modi, Madhuri Nevatia, Pushpa Gupta, Vidya Birla, and Manisha, Ashok, and Gaurang Sharma for their friendship and hospitality.

In Rādhāramaṇa Gherā, Jagadish Lāl Gosvāmī and Avinash Maharshi were especially helpful in answering my questions. I am grateful to Jagadish for permission to print some of his classic photographs. Two assistants translated the *aṣṭayama līlā* scripts with me: Brajbhushan Chaturvedi and Swapna Sharma. Swapna was also a frequent companion and a friend.

This book builds on the pioneering studies of Vrindaban bhakti by David Haberman and John Stratton (Jack) Hawley, and they have encouraged me in this enterprise. I value their friendship and have learned a great deal from both of them over the years. My debt to Jack Hawley goes far beyond this, however. He introduced me to Vrindaban, first through his writing, then by an introduction to Shrivatsa, and then as a tour guide during a quick, memorable visit to Jaisingh Ghera in 1980. His reading of the final draft of this book resulted in a number of important improvements. I thank him for his warm friendship and his frequent help.

Jamie Fuller gave a crucial nudge that started me writing. Once I had a draft of the manuscript, there were many who helped by reading and commenting on all or part of it: Cynthia Atherton, Robyn Beeche,

Gerald Boswell, Gerhard Bowering, Asimakrishna Dasa, Margaret Flinsch, Antti Pakaslahti, Karen McLean Peterson, Ludmilla Popova-Wightman, and Alan and Joan Roland. Some are familiar with this material, many are not, and their questions and comments from various perspectives have been very helpful. I thank each of them. Marston Case, Shrivatsa Goswami, Beata Grant, Dennis Hudson, Frederick Smith, and Irene Winter all read the manuscript closely. The book is much improved by their thoughtful comments and questions, though the remaining errors and omissions are, of course, my responsibility alone. Nat Case drew the plans of Jaisingh Ghera and Jaipur, and I thank him for his care and expertise.

A leave from Princeton University Press allowed me to spend three months in Vrindaban in 1991, and the press's director, Walter Lippincott, made it possible for me to retire early so that I could spend more time in India. A grant from the National Endowment for the Humanities, administered by the American Institute for Indian Studies, financed nine months of research in Vrindaban in 1994 and 1995. I am grateful to Frederick Asher, Pradip Mehendiratta, and the staff of the AIIS for their assistance and support.

At Oxford University Press, Cynthia Read has been a sympathetic editor and MaryBeth Branigan has been pleasant and professional.

Over the years my husband, Marston, encouraged my pursuit of this project, tolerated my frequent absences, and was always glad to have me back. Thank you, Marston.

Transliteration

With very few exceptions, I have used the standard transliterations from Devanāgarī script. The major exception is Krishna (Kṛṣṇa), which I have spelled in the more user-friendly fashion in response to pleas from readers not familiar with this material. Shrivatsa Goswami publishes in English using this spelling of his name; partly for the sake of convenience, I have spelled the name of his immediate family in this way, but the names of all other Gosvāmīs are spelled with diacritics. A few words that have entered the English language are spelled without diacritics. Common place-names, including Vrindaban (Vṛndāvana) are spelled as the post office does. Jaisingh Ghera is spelled without diacritics, although the name of its founder, Savāī Jayasiṃha, retains them. Those not familiar with these diacritics may safely ignore them, except to know that *ṛ* is pronounced *ri* and *ś* and *ṣ* are both pronounced *sh*. *C* is always pronounced *ch*.

CONTENTS

SEEING KRISHNA

ONE

THE COMING OF THE BLACK BEE

Seeing Krishna

The first appearance of the black bee (*bhramara*) in Jaisingh Ghera, the Goswamis' ashram on the banks of the Yamunā River in Vrindaban, was during the final hours of preparation for an *aṣṭayāma līlā*—an enactment on stage of a day in the eternal life of Krishna. An aṣṭayāma līlā is presented in eight performances, each about three hours long, around the clock on successive days. The first one starts at about 3:30 in the morning, the second at 6:00 A.M., and so on. The week-long production is a major undertaking, prepared over the course of months.[1]

The Krishna of the aṣṭayāma līlā is older than the beloved butter-stealing child of popular song and story, younger than the advisor to warriors and kings of the *Bhagavad Gītā*. Here Krishna is the playful cowherd boy, beloved son of the cowherd chief Nanda and his wife, Yaśodā, and the loving companion of the beautiful village girl, Rādhā. The time is the distant past, and now, and eternity. The place is Vrindaban, the "basil forest" (now a pilgrimage town) in the land of Vraja, the region of the north Indian plain south of Delhi and north of Agra.

The stories of Krishna's deeds in Vraja provide the material for a rich variety of the living arts all over India—painting, drama, sculpture, and dance. They have also been the basis for highly refined philosophical and theological writing; they have formed the moral framework of Vraja life and of a wider Vaiṣṇava society and provided inspiration for the rulers of the historically powerful states of Rajasthan. They are for millions of people the spiritual "glue"—as well as "lubricant"—that holds together individuals and families and eases the frictions of family life.

The stories of the early period of Krishna's life are told in the first half of the tenth canto of the *Bhāgavata Purāṇa*, probably compiled by the tenth century, and in a large corpus of poetry that is the basis of Vraja culture. The *Bhāgavata Purāṇa* is a very long scripture, even in the highly compact Sanskrit in which the original is written. It tells the history of the universe and of all the gods and heroes therein, and its longest section, the tenth canto—about one-quarter of the whole—is devoted to Krishna. Krishna was born in the ancient city of Mathura on the Yamunā River at the very end of the third era of the world cycle, the Dvāpara Yuga; his death precipitated the Kali Yuga, the fourth, degenerate age in which we live. Miraculously rescued from being killed at birth by his wicked uncle, the fearsome and jealous king Kaṁsa, he was raised by cowherds in the surrounding countryside of Vraja. The area is now virtually treeless—fields of wheat and pulses, mustard and legumes from horizon to horizon. But even a hundred years ago much of it was forested, and in Krishna's time—the distant past and eternal time—it was an idyllic landscape:

> Vrindaban was a very beautiful forest. Whatever the season, it was a delightful place. . . . The shrill chirping of the crickets was drowned by the sound of the cascading waterfalls, from which fine showers of cool water continually sprayed, making the trees around them always green. Wherever one looked, the hills were lush with the greenest grass. . . . Row upon row of trees were laden with flowers. . . . Brightly colored birds were warbling on every side, and various kinds of deer sprang about. Here peacocks uttered their shrill cry, and there bees hummed. . . . (BP X.11.35, 18.4, 5, 7)[2]

Krishna's foster father, Nanda, was chief of the cowherds. He and his wife, Yaśodā, were orthodox in their religious practices; they observed the traditional rituals and sacrifices, and they honored brahmans with lavish gifts. Starting very young, Krishna began to perform marvelous feats, defeating various demons sent by King Kaṁsa to kill him. Every time his life was in danger, Yaśodā and her friends, the other cowherd women (*gopīs*), were overcome with fear; and every time he returned safe to his mother's arms, she praised the gods and performed sacrifices for his continued safety. Although she occasionally had glimpses of his divinity, these were immediately forgotten—erased by the action of divine illusion, *māyā*—and she thought of him only as her very special, beloved child.

Krishna was a naughty boy, but his pranks were treated indulgently. When he was small, his favorite trick was to steal the butter that had been churned by his mother and the other village women.[3] When he was older, he waylaid young women who were carrying pots of curd on their head on their way to market and demanded the toll of a kiss. He stole the clothes of young women bathing in the Yamunā River, and he stole the hearts of everyone.

In fact, Krishna had one trait—besides his extraordinary feats in vanquishing demons—that led even his foster father, Nanda, and the other cowherd men to suspect that this child was very special indeed. His nature was such that all the people of Vraja loved him as if he were their own son.

When he was six, Krishna began to join his brother, Balarāma, and the other boys in taking the cows out to pasture. The boys, who played together while the cows grazed, looked to Krishna and Balarāma as their leaders. After a time, they came to trust that Krishna would get them out of any scrape they might get into. The cows, too, adored Krishna and would come running when he called them by name. And the women of the village, who eagerly awaited his return every evening, were so entranced that they came running when they heard his flute. So although Krishna's miraculous feats are the stuff that stories are made of, it was his relationship with the cowherd men and women that marked him as divine.

One of the gopīs, Rādhā, has come down in tradition as embodying to the fullest degree this special relationship of Krishna with the village people. Rādhā is nowhere mentioned by name in the *Bhāgavata Purāṇa,* but she is celebrated in Jayadeva's *Gītagovinda* (twelfth century) and the great body of devotional poetry that has grown up in the last four hundred years to celebrate Krishna's life in Vraja.[4] In this poetry, the love of Rādhā and Krishna is described in sensuous imagery. Aesthetic sensibility is understood to be inseparable from spiritual awareness, and the artistic exploration of the subtle movements of the spirit, embodied in the relationship between Rādhā and Krishna, has inspired sublime works in every medium.

As a result of this artistic abundance, the stories of Krishna's youth are readily visualized by those who hear them told. Each episode occurred in a specific place that is identified with some spot (or, often, more than one) within Vraja. Vraja is thus a sacred landscape.[5] Many of the sites are within the town of Vrindaban, which is now a busy pilgrimage center with crowded bazaars, hundreds of temples and thousands of shrines, and numerous ashrams housing both traditional holy men and modern, publicity-minded gurus. But for Krishna's devotees, the sacred basil forest that gives the town its name continues to exist. The Vrindaban where Krishna plays with his cowherd friends is an aspect of reality that is in constant interaction with the mundane world.

Krishna's activity is called *līlā*—literally, play. He performed all his youthful feats in play, just for the fun of it. The pleasure that he felt in his actions was the pure pleasure of eternal bliss, and the līlās not only took place in the context of the lives of his human companions (or were they manifestations of gods?) but also were the activity of cosmic being and consciousness, creating the universe. To hear or see Krishna's līlās is thus to glimpse a way out of the conditions of life imposed by karma. For the devotee, the līlās narrated in the *Bhāgavata Purāṇa* are taken as having happened historically, but they also happen eternally. Krishna participates in the recurring daily, monthly, and yearly patterns of the natural world, and his devotees can also participate in his activities in this eternal realm, through visualization, development of a refined emotional involvement in the stories, and service to those who are placed in a position to be served.[6]

There is one stretch of the riverbank of the Yamunā that is understood by many devotees to be the setting for a daily līlā in the eternal Vrindaban. Here Krishna and Rādhā are visualized as arriving by riverboat each evening (from where is not specified) to prepare for their nightly tryst. Most vividly imaged is Rādhā, who, after landing, bathes and is dressed and ornamented by her eight attendants (*sakhīs*). Krishna, somewhat less clearly imagined, also lands, is served by the attendants, and prepares himself. The two lovers then retire to a bower to rest before they begin an evening of dance and games with their friends and eventually retire for their ultimate union.

This same spot on the Yamunā is also the location of the final event in the *Bhāgavata Purāṇa*'s story of Krishna's years in Vrindaban. When, in time, Krishna had to leave the scenes of his happy youth and slay the usurping king of Mathura, he left behind the village women whom he had teased, flirted with, and entranced. They were inconsolable, and their grief at being separated from Krishna was intensified by stories reaching them that he was dallying with the fine ladies of Mathura. Krishna, knowing the distress of his parents and of the women of Vraja, sent his most trusted companion, the highly accomplished intellectual and philosopher Uddhava, to console them. He arrived one evening, and the next morning the village women saw that a stranger had come during the night and was staying in Nanda's house. They waited until Uddhava returned from taking his bath in the Yamunā and then greeted him. The *Bhāgavata Purāṇa* tells what happened next:

> The women were astonished to see that he looked so much like Śrī Krishna. His long arms came to his knees, his eyes were as soft as newly opened lotuses, he was dressed in yellow silk, and on his neck hung a garland of blue lotus flowers. (BP X.47.1)

> His jewel-studded earrings shimmered, and his face shone like a lotus. The blessed women, smiling, said to one another, "This man is very beautiful to look at. But who is he? Where is he from? Whose messenger is he? Why is he dressed like Śrī Krishna?" And, curious to meet him, they eagerly gathered around that friend and servant of Śrī Krishna who had taken refuge in the lotus feet of the most excellent Lord. (2)
>
> Guessing that he had come with a message from Śrī Krishna, the women received Uddhava respectfully, bending low before him and greeting him with smiles and modest glances, with friendly words and other signs of welcome. They showed him to a secluded seat, and then began to question him. (3)

Devotees believe that this secluded spot was the same place that Krishna eternally lands for his nightly trysts. Despite their civility to Uddhava, the women's words reflected their bitterness at Krishna's departure:

> "We know who you are: you are a senior minister of the leader of the Yadavas, and you have graced this place by coming here, bearing his message. Your Master sent you here to bring pleasure to his father and mother. (4)
>
> "There is nothing else that we can think of that he might remember in this village of cows and cowherds. Even very great sages have difficulty letting go the ties of love that bind them to their mother and father and other family members. (5)
>
> "But ties of affection with anyone else are a sham, born of self-interest alone, and last only as long as the motive remains—like the attraction of black bees to flowers or the love between men and women. (6)
>
> "When a prostitute comes to know that the man who visits her has no more money, she drops him; when subjects see that their ruler cannot protect them, they abandon him; when students have completed their studies, will they continue to serve their spiritual teacher? Priests conducting a sacrifice depart when they have received their fees. (7)
>
> "When no fruit remains on a tree, birds fly away without a thought; guests leave a house after they have eaten; deer flee from a forest that is on fire. And the seducer will abandon a woman once he has possessed her, however much she loves him." (8)
>
> Thus the women, whose speech and body and heart were dedicated to Govinda, forgot themselves completely and spoke without shame to Śrī Krishna's messenger when he arrived in Vraja. (9)
>
> And still they continued to remember the many līlās of their Beloved, and sang of them again and again. Oblivious of themselves and forgetting all sense of womanly modesty, they wept bitterly as they recalled his childhood and youthful deeds. (10)

At this point Uddhava, greatly impressed by the devotion of the women, had the impulse to touch the feet of a gopī (whom popular tradition takes to be Rādhā) in respect—a gesture that would be quite extraordinary for a man of his class and attainments. Tradition also names Rādhā as the one who speaks next:

> One of them, absorbed in thoughts of sporting with the Beloved, saw a black bee humming nearby, and understood it to be a messenger of Śrī Krishna. She began to speak to it: (11)
>
> "O you who suck honey, you are a friend of the Fraud, and you also are a fraud. Do not dare to touch our feet in deceitful greeting, or try to persuade us with your pleas. We see that your moustaches have been smeared with the bright yellow saffron painted on the breasts of our rivals, which clung to the flower garlands worn by Śrī Krishna when he embraced them. You, too, fly here and there making love to one flower after another. Let the leader of the Madhavas himself—he whose messenger you are—come to show us the token of those proud ladies' favor, which would be laughed at among the Yadavas. Did he have to send you to do this for him? (12)
>
> "You are black, and so is he. When you have sucked the juice from flowers, you fly away, as he also left us, innocent cowherd women. Just once he let us taste the bewitching and completely intoxicating nectar on his lips, and then he deserted us. I don't know how Lakṣmī, goddess of good fortune, can continue to adore his lotus feet. Her heart must have been captured by the honeyed words of that charmer, Śrī Krishna. (13)
>
> "O six-legged one, why do you keep humming the praises of this chief of the Yadavas to us, who knew him long ago? We left our homes to live in the forest because of those old, familiar stories. Why do you sing them to us again and again? Your flattery will not get you anywhere with us. Go away, go sing to the ladies whom Arjuna's friend now loves; they are new, they don't know the stories as we do. He has soothed the agony of their hearts, and your flatteries will please them. They will give you what you ask for." (14)

It does not matter in this self-reflexive story in which there is no "before" and "after" that Krishna's encounter with the warrior Arjuna (and the dialogue of the *Bhagavad Gītā*) does not occur until Krishna has been gone much longer from Vrindaban. Rādhā continues:

> "O black bee! Is there a woman anywhere who, once she has surrendered to the treacherous charm of his smile and graceful movements of his eyebrows, could ever leave his side? No! There is not one such woman in heaven, on earth, or in deepest hell. When Lakṣmī herself worships the dust of his feet, what are we to him? When you return to him, tell him that though many good people call him Uttamaśloka—'He whose glories are to be sung'—this name is a mockery. (15)
>
> "O honeyed one! Don't rub your head on my feet! I know full well that you have learned from Mukunda [Krishna] the art of winning hearts

> with beautiful words and diplomatic ploys, and have come here as his messenger. But your persuasions will not work on us. For him we left behind our children, husbands, and the opinion of others—and then he left us with a light heart, not even slightly grateful! How can we understand such ingratitude? How can we trust him now? (16)
>
> ". . . Now, go away. We have no use for Krishna or any black-robed minister of his. But if you ask us why we continue to talk about him, we would have to tell the truth. Once an addiction for him has been formed, it's impossible to let it go; even if we wished, we could not stop talking of him. (17)
>
> "For the recitation of his deeds, of his sports, is ambrosia to the ear; many men, who simply by tasting a single drop of these stories are freed from the difficulties of life—that interplay between pairs of opposites—and thereupon die to the ordinary world, suddenly leave the miserable concerns of family and lead here on earth the life of religious mendicants, like so many birds. (18)
>
> "We believed the words of this Fraud to be true, like the wives of the black buck, who are foolishly charmed by love when they hear the hunter's song, and then are pierced by his arrows. In just this way we, the companions of this dark one, experienced more than once the sharp pains of love from the touch of his nails. Therefore, O messenger, now speak of something else." (19)

But then, in a change of mood, Rādhā speaks more wistfully:

> "Have you, then, come back, O friend of the Beloved? Did he send you? Ask what you wish of us—we must oblige, O messenger! Is there some way you can take us to him whose embrace it is so difficult to be without? His bride, the beautiful Lakṣmī, lying in the form of a curl of golden hair on his very chest, is always with him. (20)

Lakṣmī, the goddess of prosperity, is said to reside in a golden curl of hair (*śrīvatsa*) on Krishna's chest, so as never to be separated from him. Rādhā continues:

> "Tell me, is my lord and master now in Mathura? O gentle one, does he remember his father's house and those who have been close to him, and the gopīs? Does he ever talk of us, his servants? O when will he put his arm, more fragrant than aloe wood, on my head?" (21)

Devotees believe that the black bee was Krishna himself, who could not bear the separation from his beloved Rādhā, and who came to enable Uddhava to express his newfound devotion.

Uddhava, intellectual and master of yogic discipline, was deeply moved by the women's words. The night before, he had consoled Krishna's mother and father by telling them that they were very blessed to have known Krishna as a son, and offered hope to them that they would see him soon again (though we, on hearing his words, know that Krishna never did return to Vrindaban, and that if his parents saw their son it was only in their hearts). Uddhava now began to talk to the women in a similar vein, in terms that have traditionally been used to praise devotion as a surer path than asceticism or ritual alone in this age of darkness.

> "Most surely your wishes have been fulfilled; the entire world honors you, for you have given your hearts so fully to the Lord Vāsudeva. (23)
>
> "Others can only attain devotion to Śrī Krishna through the strength of charitable giving, the strength of fasting and austerities, of sacrifices and prayers, the strength of studying the Vedas, controlling the senses, and performing the most varied of meritorious acts. (24)
>
> "You have reached the highest degree of devotion to Bhagavān, the Lord of supreme renown—a blissful state that even the sages find it hard to reach. (25)
>
> "O bliss, that for him you have sacrificed sons, husbands, bodies, families, and homes, and have chosen the Supreme Person, whose name is Krishna." (26)

Then he acknowledges that he himself has learned from their devoted longing in separation:

> "You have bestowed on Śrī Krishna all that fills your soul; and your separation from him has done me a great favor, O privileged ones! (27)
>
> "Listen to the message I have brought from the Beloved, which will fill your hearts with joy, for he confides his secrets in me. (28)
>
> "The Lord said: 'You can never be completely separated from me. Just as the five elements—ether, air, fire, water, and earth—are present in everything that exists, so am I present in the mind and heart, the vital breath, the elements, the senses of perception, and the organs of action, as well as the three qualities.'" (29)

The three "qualities" (*guṇa,* also translated as "virtues" when applied to a person) are the fundamental characteristics of light, heat, and cold or darkness; or alternatively serenity, passion, and hatred; or any of various other trinities of attributes. They are fundamental constituents of the universe, from which the action of māyā, or creative energy, constitutes the phenomenal world. Uddhava continues with his metaphysical discourse:

> "'For in the creation, maintenance, and destruction of the worlds, I am the doer and that which is done, and it all occurs within myself, for the elements, the senses, and the qualities are all activated by the power of my own creative energy. (30)

> "'The essence of the soul is knowledge; it is pure, transcendent, unconnected with the qualities. It may be perceived in deep sleep, or in dreams, or while awake, thanks to the power of my creative energy acting on the individual's heart and mind. (31)
>
> "'In order to recognize that the objects of the senses are unreal—just as when a man wakes up he realizes that his dream was not reality—a man should know that within himself which confuses his real self with his senses. (32)
>
> "'The Vedas, the teachings of Yoga and Sāṃkhya, renunciation, asceticism, subjugation of the senses, and the cultivation of truthfulness—all these flow toward the goal of recognizing that what the senses perceive is unreal, just as rivers flow toward the sea."' (33)

But it is not for the women—or most humans—to seek to know that their world is metaphysically unreal. Their task is to cultivate devotion, the only path to knowledge of the truth, and thus salvation, in this age. Thus the message from Krishna offers more immediate personal counseling, indicating the path of the devotee:

> "'I have removed myself from you so that you will fix your mind on me, your Beloved, and will come near me in your thoughts. (34)
>
> "'A woman's thoughts are fixed on her beloved when he is far away much more than when he stays close by and within her sight. (35)
>
> "'Concentrate on me all the strength of your soul, let go the movement of all other thoughts, remember me constantly, and you will be reunited with me before long.'"(36)

We get a mixed message about what happened next, as the text seems to struggle between two versions of the story. On the one hand, the women are reconciled to Krishna's departure and wish him happiness:

> The women of Vraja, on hearing the message brought by Uddhava, which awakened their memories of the Beloved, said to him joyfully: (38)
>
> "It's very fortunate that he has killed the wicked King Kaṁsa and all his retinue, who gave the Yadavas such trouble, and that now he is happily surrounded by friends and family who have regained all their worldly goods—this also is most fortunate." (39)

On the other hand, they are well aware that the message Uddhava brings will not cure them of their longing, and they continue to be jealous:

> "O gentle one, tell us if Krishna brings delight to the beautiful women of Mathura, as he did to us who welcomed him with shy smiles full of love and adored him with bashful glances. Is it true that in the same way Krishna brings pleasure to the beautiful women of the city, who welcome him with bashful glances? (40)

"How could he who is skilled in the games of love and is beloved by the most beautiful women—how could he not be captivated by their respectful words and loving gestures? (41)

"O pious one, when he is relaxed and talking freely of old times, surrounded by city ladies, does he ever remember us, cowherd women of the village? (42)

"Does Govinda [Krishna] ever remember those nights under a full moon in the forest of Vrindaban, where the lotus and jasmine were blooming, when it pleased him, in the great circle dance, to mark the rhythm with the clink of bells encircling his ankles, while we sang the stories of his great deeds, which enchant the heart? (43)

"Will he who is the source of our suffering and our tears ever return here and restore life to us by the touch of his limbs, as Indra restores life to the forest when the rain clouds brush over it? (44)

"Why should Krishna come back here, now that he has conquered a kingdom, slain his enemies, married the daughters of many kings, and is most happily surrounded by the ones he loves? (45)

"What need does this great soul, spouse of Lakṣmī, have of us who live in the forest, or even of those other women? All his desires are fulfilled and his Person is perfect and self-contained. (46)

"The courtesan Piṅgalā said that the height of happiness is to have lost all desire; we know this, and yet we cannot help but wish to meet him. (47)

"Who would have the courage to let go all thoughts of the secret encounters with the One whose glory is so great—when, in spite of herself, Lakṣmī never leaves his Person? (48)

"River, mountain, woodlands, cows, the sound of the flute—everything here, O mighty Uddhava, that was connected with Krishna and his companion Saṁkarṣaṇa [Balarāma] remind us constantly of the cowherd Nanda's son, and in the presence of his hallowed footprints, we cannot forget him. (49–50)

"When our hearts have been captured by his graceful walk, his joyful laughter, and sweet words, how could we forget him, O Uddhava? (51)

"O Lord . . . O you who protect Vraja and destroy suffering, O Govinda, rescue Vraja from the ocean of agony into which it has plunged!" (52)

This is the cry of longing in separation that has echoed through the centuries in the devotional poetry of India. But the text glosses over the women's agony:

> Thus hearing Krishna's message cured the women of the feverish suffering caused by separation from him; they recognized him to be their very Self, and respectfully welcomed Uddhava. (53)
>
> Krishna's messenger stayed among the cowherd women for several months, dispelling their sadness and bringing delight to Vraja by singing the stories of Krishna's deeds. (54)

Popular tradition has it, however, that it was the women who taught Uddhava during these months. Having known the joy of feeding him, serving him, and dancing with him in the great circle dance, their agony of separation from him kept them constantly mindful of his appearance, his smiles, his activities (*līlās*). He was alive to them as he was not to the philosopher and intellectual, however much Uddhava was devoted to Krishna in his way, and when Uddhava recognized this, he could learn from them.

This stretch of the bank of the Yamunā is thus given stories in eternal time and in the golden days of Krishna's lifetime. But remains of buildings along the river bring us somewhat closer, into historical time. Bricks that date to the Mauryan period, about the third century B.C.E., have been found less than a mile upstream from the place where Rādhā talked to the black bee, in the foundation of the present temple of Madanamohana on the banks of the Yamunā. In the third century B.C.E., the nearby city of Mathura was a thriving center, and there was probably a settlement in Vrindaban. But we know little about the site until the sixteenth century. In 1515 C.E., Vrindaban was again a virtually uninhabited forest when the Bengali saint Śrī Caitanya Mahāprabhu visited this land of Krishna's idylls.[7] Here he identified many of the sites of Krishna's līlās, and over the years other holy men identified others.[8] Those who follow the Caitanyaite tradition believe that the saint used to sit for his spiritual exercises near the place where Rādhā and Krishna had come for their trysts.

Caitanya charged six of his ablest followers, later called the Six Gosvāmīs, to establish Vrindaban as a center of devotion to Krishna. Temples were built, and small groups of Caitanya's followers settled here and in nearby places in Vraja.[9]

About two hundred years later, Rāja Savāī Jayasiṃha (Jaisingh) of Āmera (Amber), one of the most powerful ministers of the Mughal emperor Aurangzeb and a devout worshiper of Rādhā and Krishna, established a retreat for himself in Vrindaban while he was governor of the Mughal province of Agra. The site he chose was on the riverbank where Rādhā and Krishna trysted and where Caitanya used to sit. He acquired six parcels of land, about two and a half acres altogether, where he constructed a house for himself; a pavilion on the river front, where Caitanya had sat; behind it, a shrine to Caitanya and two of his close companions; steps leading down to the river at the divine couple's landing places; and a temple for his personal deity, Nṛtya Gopāla (see plan, Figure 1). Beside his house, he built a large platform where *rāsalīlās,* musical dance dramas depicting the activities of Krishna and his companions, were performed.

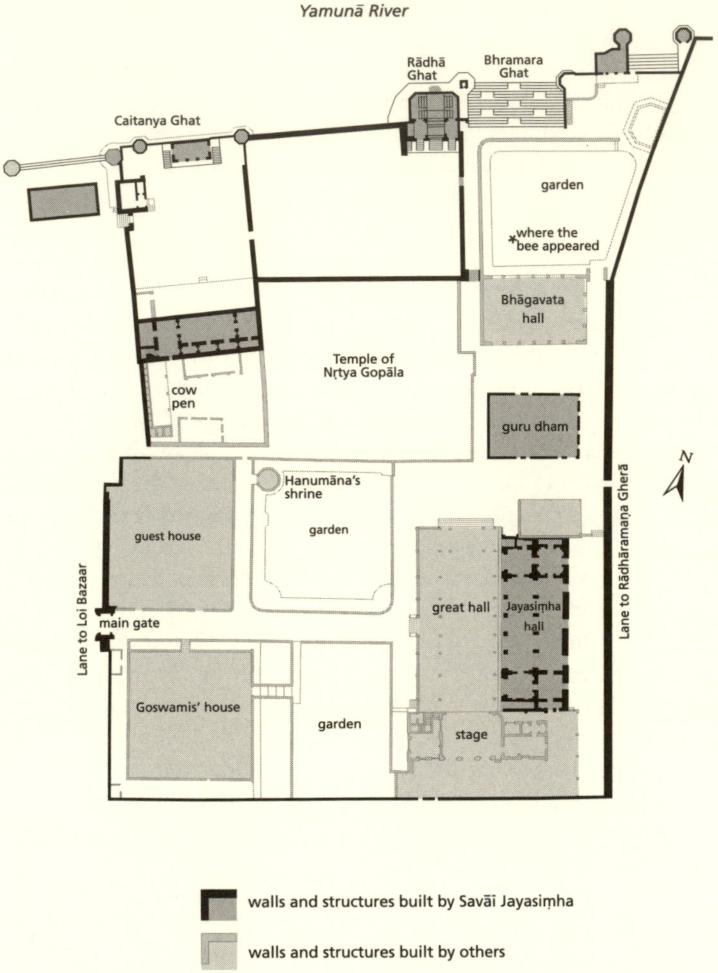

Figure 1. Plan of Jaisingh Ghera. Drawing by Nat Case.

The Goswami family, who now live on the property, reason that Savāī Jayasiṃha must have stayed here whenever he could for twenty-odd years, and it is known that he attracted notable philosophers, artists, and scholars here, making it a spiritual and cultural center.[10] He sponsored within his compound a periodic rāsalīlā festival, with the support of the mahārājas of Kotah and Jodhpur; this was the first time that theatrical performances of rāsalīlās were performed outside temple auspices in Vraja. It was probably in this compound that he planned the new city of Jaipur, built in the early eighteenth century, and the great astronomical observatories, the *jantar mantar*, for which he is widely known. In any case, Savāī Jayasiṃha was not only an outstanding soldier and administrator, astronomer and scholar, but also a connoisseur, patron, and devotee of Vraja.

The compound as a whole came to be known as Jaisingh Ghera (or Jayasiṃha Gherā), and today the buildings are still standing. In this century, part of the land was used as a wrestling ground; the wrestlers worshiped their patron deity Hanumān in a small shrine established next to the rāsalīlā platform by Savāī Jayasiṃha in 1699.[11] After Independence, the compound was auctioned off by the government of Rajasthan and came into the possession of Śrī Puruṣottama Gosvāmī Mahārāja ("Mahārāj jī"), a priest in the service of the nearby Rādhāramaṇa temple. Under his direction, Savāī Jayasiṃha's rāsalīlā platform was transformed into a great hall with a proscenium stage for the performance of rāsalīlās and other traditional dance and music. Over Savāī Jayasiṃha's residence and the performance hall were built accommodations for devotees and visiting scholars. A library and other facilities for research were established over the course of two or three decades, and Jaisingh Ghera once again became an important cultural center, sponsoring many of the traditional Vaiṣṇava arts of Vraja. (A Vaiṣṇava here may be taken to mean one who reveres Krishna as the highest deity. The word more generally means a worshiper of Viṣṇu in his various forms, which most notably include, besides Krishna, Rāma, the protagonist of the *Rāmāyaṇa*.)

Part of the property along the river had been leased by the Rajasthan government to a small school, and because of Indian tenancy laws, this area could not be used by the Goswamis until some agreement could be reached with the tenants. In the summer of 1992, the school was at last vacated, and Jaisingh Ghera was once again virtually complete, lacking only the temple built by Savāī Jayasiṃha for Nṛtya Gopāla in the center of the compound. This remained in the hands of the Rajasthan government, for temples cannot be bought and sold. (A passageway from the street to this temple permits access to it without entering Jaisingh Ghera, and it is a stop on the regular pilgrim tour of sacred sites in Vrindaban.) During the monsoon that year, when the Yamunā rose to the height of the banks along the river, excavations were begun, uncovering the structures that Savāī Jayasiṃha had built to accommodate the nightly landing of the divine couple.

Krishna's landing place consists of a flight of stone steps (*ghāṭa* or ghat) down to the level that must once have been the Yamunā's shore.

Punctuating the stairs are nine platforms—a larger central one for Krishna to stand on and eight smaller ones, on different levels, for the eight attendants. Was this in Savāī Jayasiṃha's time perhaps the setting for an enactment of Krishna's evening activities? Separated from Krishna's space by a wall through which there is a small doorway, Rādhā's space includes a covered flight of stairs leading down to a small pool protected by high walls, which form half an octagon. Halfway up the stairs, also under the roof, there is a small room to one side, where Rādhā could be dressed and adorned by her friends. The stairs leading into the pool also number eight—one for each of the attendants.

Excavation of the river front coincided with preparations for the staging of an aṣṭayāma līlā in the performance hall of Jaisingh Ghera in the autumn of 1992. Various dimensions of this eight-day drama are explored at greater length in the following chapters, for an aṣṭayāma līlā is not merely a performance, but a process of revealing the reality of the eternal world. Before the līlā could begin, therefore, it was necessary to invoke the eternal performers. On the morning of October 29, a worship service (*pūjā*) was performed at Krishna's landing place—also called Bhramara ghat (black bee's stairs)—by the Goswamis' family priest, Ācārya Prāṇa Gopāla Miśra, who performs all of their public and life-cycle rituals. The family and perhaps a hundred devotees who had come from all over the country for the aṣṭayāma līlā sat on the steps of the ghat during the ceremony. Then the Goswamis and the devotees went through the doorway in the wall to Rādhā's ghat. There pūjā was again performed.

That evening, the deity was evoked in the performance hall by the dancer Birju Mahārāj, whose choreography for the occasion was based on the text of the *Govindalīlāmṛtam* (Ambrosia of the Sport of Govinda [Krishna]).[12] This poetic text, which also provided the framework for the script of the aṣṭayāma līlā, describes a day in the life of Krishna in the eternal Vrindaban.

The whole next day was devoted to a more intense preparation. For the entire twenty-four hours, a relay team of Vaiṣṇavas chanted the *mahāmantra* (great mantra): "Haré Krishna, Haré Krishna, Krishna, Krishna, Haré, Haré; Haré Rāma, Haré Rāma, Rāma, Rāma, Haré, Haré," marking out time and space with names of the deity. Around-the-clock recitation of the *Bhāgavata Purāṇa* at Bhramara ghat was begun that day.

Blessings by the spiritual personages of Vrindaban were also arranged. Five groups of thirty-one brahmans and others were invited to come during the morning and afternoon and be honored by Mahārāj jī: ritual priests, scholars of the *Bhāgavata Purāṇa*, secular scholars and teachers, pilgrim guides, and the men and boys who would be performing the rāsalīlās. All were male; the ritual aspects of Caitanyaite Vaiṣṇavism, especially in Rādhāramaṇa temple, remain staunchly conservative, although in many other respects that temple has led the way in opening up to the modern world. Each participant was ceremonially greeted by Mahārāj jī, assisted by his sons, Shrivatsa and Veṇu Gopāla, who washed their feet and presented them with yellow cloths to wear. Each then spoke briefly about Bhramara ghat and its significance. The whole event was recorded by a professional video team to be preserved as part of the ashram's archives.

These ceremonies all took place under a large white tent (*pāṇḍala*) that covered the open space behind Bhramara ghat, including the site traditionally believed to be the bower where Krishna and Rādhā rested after adorning themselves for their tryst. On the rear wall of the tent was a large painted hanging that had been created especially for the occasion; it depicted Rādhā and her companions under a tree, staring at a large black bee at Rādhā's feet (Figure 2).

After dark had fallen, when all the men had spoken, Mahārāj jī asked one of his devotees, Sonal Mansingh, a gifted dancer, to speak. She was

Figure 2. Rādhā addressing the black bee. Painting on cloth by Bihari Lal Chaturvedi; photo by Robyn Beeche.

the only woman to have taken the microphone that day (Figure 3). As she began her invocation, a large black beetle, about two inches long, flew into the tent from the direction of the river and landed on the ground in front of her. Astounded, those devotees who were close enough to see what was going on rose to their feet, exclaiming "Jai ho!" and "Jai Śrī Rādhé!"—literally, "Let there be victory!" and "Victory to Rādhā!" exclamations of acclaim and approval used generally in Vrindaban. But how could a black beetle be understood immediately as the same as the black bee of the *Bhāgavata Purāṇa*? It will be clear at several points in this book that things are often understood as both one thing and another, at the same time—*acintyabhedābheda,* inconceivable difference in nondifference.[13]

The visitor danced on the ground and flew up to dance in the air, alighting two or three more times—long enough to be captured on video—before flying off again toward the river. Mahārāj jī, deeply moved, spoke, saying that the divine spirit can take any form, and for those who could see with devotion and love, it was Krishna's presence that had become visible. Encouraged by the other leaders and priests present, he declared that a beautiful bower would be created to commemorate this manifestation. He also declared that he would not leave Vrindaban for a year and that the *Bhāgavata Purāṇa* would be reads daily on this spot for perpetuity.[14]

The devotees who had gathered in Jaisingh Ghera for the aṣṭayāma līlā, although sincere believers, were also people who live in this ordinary world, and the general reaction that evening and the next day was happiness, but not complete acceptance that a miracle had occurred. A wonderful, unusual event, yes—the appearance of this visitor, never before seen in this area, with such perfect timing—but to accept fully that this was a manifestation of divinity was difficult. Trying to help his followers absorb what had happened, Mahārāj jī told the devotees that four factors contributed to this miracle: first, this was the site of the original bhramara's appearance; second, the deity was summoned by the devotion of the people gathered there; third, this was the site of the eternal aṣṭayāma līlā; and fourth, the day of the bee's appearance had been spent in concentrated spiritual activity by the 155 honored guests, which had summoned the black bee.

One can recognize here elements of both devotionalism and the logic of ritual performance, by which it is believed that there is such power in words rightly said and rituals rightly performed (by those who are qualified) that the universe itself is affected. As Mahārāj jī's son Shrivatsa later explained, the world, which is the body of God, can be

Figure 3. Sonal Mansingh speaking, just before the black bee appeared.

shaped by that unique physical property which is all-pervasive and immutable: sound. God can be invoked through sound and, in fact, is incarnated only when invoked. The invoking sound is the mantra, and when the mahāmantra ("Haré Krishna, Haré Krishna . . .") was sounded in the context of that place and that time, in the midst of the devotion of all present, the deity had no choice but to appear—and in the form of a bee, his authentic form in that context.

Right on schedule, at 3:36 in the early morning of the following day, the aṣṭayāma līlā began in the great hall, watched by a packed house of about 1,500 enthusiastic devotees of Krishna. The next night, the second līlā began at 6:00 in the morning. This was a day in the lunar ritual calendar that is considered a time when any action taken will not decay (*akṣaya navamī*). So Mahārāj jī had decided to consecrate the site of the bower that evening. An octagonal platform was prepared from the sand of the Yamunā River, on which were placed small figurines of Rādhā's eight companions, as well as flowers, banana-pith carvings, and auspicious patterns drawn with colored powders. In the center was an eight-petaled lotus made of banana pith.

To dedicate a shrine to a deity, an image is needed. A Polaroid photograph had been made from the videotape of the black bee, placed in a silver frame, and kept to one side until the priest would need it. During the first part of the ritual, all went as planned. But then, as the ritual specialists were reciting their mantras in powerful voices that resounded through the pavilion, and just at the moment when the priest asked Mahārāj jī for the photograph of the bee to be placed on the lotus in the middle of the platform, the bhramara itself appeared. It flew in again from the north and landed on the ground next to the octagonal platform, opposite the priests. A devotee picked it up carefully on a leaf and placed it on the platform, where it walked directly to the central lotus, and installed itself underneath the flower. There it stayed quietly throughout the rest of the ceremony.

Pandemonium broke out. This time everyone saw the visitor and shouted and pushed to come closer. The consecration ceremony continued, and after things had quieted down a bit, Mahārāj jī led the chanting devotees in circumambulating the platform, transforming the bedlam into ecstatic celebration. Meanwhile, a brahman sat quietly a few yards away, continuing to read the chapters of the *Bhāgavata Purāṇa*. Throughout that evening and the next day, the conviction was strengthened among the devotees that the bhramara's perfectly timed appearance and precisely appropriate behavior signified a manifestation of Krishna.

The bhramara appeared yet again two days later, on the night when the gods are awakened from their four-month sleep during the monsoon season (*devotthāna ekādaśī*). This was the first occasion on which the newly established shrine was used for a regular ritual observance. A small group had gathered in the white tent for the pūjā, and a few of the women were singing devotional songs at the end of the ritual. The black bee flew in from the river again, and as the group stood to watch, it flew just over our heads and among the lights under the tent. Every so often, it stopped and rested behind the group, and then flew again, around the lights. After several minutes, Mahārāj jī said the lights should be turned off and the group should disperse. The black bee was never seen again.

The story was told and retold in the months and years to come. The videotape was eagerly viewed by visitors to the ashram. One small detail was changed in the retelling, however—it was said that on its second visit the bhramara landed directly on the platform, not that it landed beside it and was helped up by a devotee. The video footage that showed it being lifted up was edited out. For many Westerners who hear the story, this jumps out as the most interesting part of it—aha! Doctoring the evidence to fortify belief! A somewhat more analytic—and sympathetic—view brings to bear another question: what exactly is meant by "seeing" the divinity in this context? Where are we? Are we in the traditional story of the coming of the black bee, or in the twentieth century, documenting a celebration on video? But why either/or? Is not the truth both/and? And if the truth is both/and, what may be lost in factuality is gained in emphasizing the congruence between the two worlds. Certain details, "factual" though they might be, detract from the "reality" of what is seen. The process may be broadly compared with the formation of a traditional icon, which may be anatomically improbable, but which conveys a way of seeing that points to awareness of the coexistence of two worlds.

TWO

MAHĀRĀJ JĪ

The coming of the black bee was for Mahārāj jī the climax of a lifetime of effort, dedicated to devotion of Krishna.[1] He was born in the lineage of priests—now encompassing forty-two families—of Rādhāramaṇa temple, one of the original temples of Vrindaban founded by the Six Gosvāmīs in the sixteenth century, and his birth in this lineage was an essential prerequisite for his vocation. He inherited from his father a network of devotees who had over time supported his family. He was also born with intelligence, abundant energy, and a good voice. His achievements build on these gifts but are, above all, evidence of his self-discipline and his creativity, grounded in his unswerving pursuit of service to the deity.

Life

Mahārāj jī's earliest years were spent in Rādhāramaṇa Gherā, the walled compound enclosing about thirty tightly packed, two-story houses around the temple of Rādhāramaṇa. His father was a respected guru who followed the family tradition of serving Rādhāramaṇa and giving spiritual counsel to disciples, although his talent was in singing, not in giving public discourses. (His own father, Mahārāj jī's grandfather, had been a renowned scholar of the *Bhāgavata Purāṇa* and a teacher.) Mahārāj jī's father enjoyed the income from property in Patna, given by a devotee, and he divided his time between Patna, Varanasi (where the family had long been established), and Vrindaban. He was a wrestler and loved the pleasures of food and company; by his lifestyle he attracted the sobriquet Rāja jī, or King, which made it all the more natural to address his learned son as Mahārāj jī.[2] Mahārāj jī's father had one daughter and no sons by his first wife. When it became clear that she would not bear any sons to continue the lineage, she took the initiative in arranging for him to marry a second time. His second wife bore him two daughters and three sons. Mahārāj jī's father died suddenly and peacefully, presumably of a massive heart attack, when he was about thirty-nine, leaving six children, the third child and oldest boy being Puruṣottama (now Mahārāj jī), eight years old.

Mahārāj jī attended school in Vrindaban until he was eighteen, when he went to Varanasi. The family had had connections with Varanasi for some three hundred years; among their connections was a family of devotees living about five miles from the city, who gave the young man a place to live. The renowned scholar Sārvabhauma Gosvāmī Śrīdāmodara Lāla Śāstrī—a Rādhāramaṇa Gosvāmī of Mahārāj jī's grandfather's generation—was living there, and Mahārāj jī attached himself to the service of this great man. He used to get up before dawn to eat breakfast and walk or take a rickshaw to the old man's house, arriving there by eight in the morning. He stayed, serving his teacher, until midnight and, it is said, did not eat again until he had left his guru's house. At first, he was not taught directly. The old man refused to teach him, saying "don't come here, go to some school, you are wasting your time here." Mahārāj jī persisted, pulling the chain of the cloth ceiling fan over his teacher all day long in the hot weather, listening as others were being taught, and walking home late at night. Finally, having proved his determination, he was accepted as a student.

For their living, the Gosvāmīs of Rādhāramaṇa temple have always, until very recent times, been supported entirely by the offerings of devotees. In the twentieth century, they began to widen their circle of supporters by giving public discourses on the *Bhāgavata Purāṇa*, thereby attracting more followers.

Shortly after Mahārāj jī's father died, the family in Vrindaban was robbed of all its property and possessions by a trusted family retainer and left destitute. So as soon as possible, the young man began his own career along the traditional lines, and he turned out to be a natural preacher. The network of the family's devotees and supporters all over the country invited him to give discourses, and he was in great demand. Out of respect, he refused all requests to preach in Varanasi, however, so long as his own guru was alive. He was with his guru for twelve years

Figure 4. Mahārāj jī as a young guru, in the 1950s. Photo by Bharat Studios, Mathura.

until the latter's death in 1949, living some of this time in Vrindaban but most of the time apart from his family, studying, practicing his devotion, and giving discourses (see Figure 4).

When he was nineteen, Mahārāj jī married, and soon thereafter, wishing to follow the example of Śrī Caitanya Mahāprabhu (whom we shall meet at greater length in chapter 4), he shaved his head and vowed never to wear a sewn garment. From this age onward, he always dressed in vivid orange—understood to be a shade of Krishna's yellow, not a shade of the traditional ocher or saffron of the renunciant. Although he remained a householder, he set himself a strict regimen of discipline and study, through which he developed his understanding of devotion to the deity and ability to practice it. One practice, for example, was to read aloud (or under the breath) the entire *Bhāgavata Purāṇa* in a week, in one or at most two sessions each day, for a total of six or seven hours a day (*saptāha pārāyaṇa*). This must be done in a state of purity, and one cannot eat, drink, or use the toilet while doing the reading. When undertaken in the midst of an already full and busy life, it requires considerable endurance and self-discipline.

There is a story of Mahārāj jī's powers over himself and others that dates to this period. One evening, when he was twenty-one years old—his oldest child was six months old—when Mahārāj jī returned home from evening worship at Rādhāramaṇa temple, he found two men waiting at the door of his house. They said they came from a village near Gwalior and wanted to take Mahārāj jī with them to do a seven-day *Bhāgavata* discourse at the Hanumān temple there. The priest of that temple had heard that this young man gave excellent discourses and was urgently inviting him to come. Mahārāj jī objected that he was already scheduled to give a discourse somewhere else, but they asked, who should have priority, some businessman or Hanumān? Mahārāj jī, of course, said that Hanumān should, so he agreed to go along with them the next day. Mahārāj jī's mother tried to intervene, saying that he should not go with complete strangers, but the men promised his safety, and he went with them.

The next morning Mahārāj jī left, taking with him for company and assistance the lean and elderly family retainer Śarma jī. They went by bus to a remote village near Gwalior, where there was a Hanumān temple served by a couple of sādhus. A small crowd attended his discourse the first day, but the crowd grew each day, attracting people from villages all around the area.

On the last day, a few people came there with some camels, and said to Mahārāj jī, "O pandit, you have to come with us, now." Mahārāj jī objected, saying that he was already behind in his obligations. But the men insisted, saying, "No one ever says no to us—though because you are a pandit, we are handling you lightly." Mahārāj jī asked the sādhu, "What is this? You promised me safety." "Yes," said the sādhu, "I can get you safely to the bus stop or the railway station, but these people will be able to get you there or anywhere else." "Who are they?" asked Mahārāj jī. "I cannot say," said the sādhu. So Mahārāj jī resigned himself to going, and Śarma went with him, although the old man was sick with fear and developed uncontrollable diarrhea.

So the next morning, Mahārāj jī got on one camel, Śarma (half-dead) on another, and they were blindfolded and led for hours through the ravines of the Cambala River—a region notorious as the hideout of robber bands. When they reached their destination, another village, they were housed with a brahman family, and the discourse started peacefully. Everything seemed quiet, but no one would talk to them or socialize.

On the fifth day of the discourse, when Mahārāj jī was out early in the morning for his ablutions, he happened to meet his host, the brahman, in a secluded place. He asked him quietly why he kept two guns in his room: "What ablutions do you make with guns?" The brahman replied, "Don't you know? This is Rāja Man Singh's village, and no one asks questions." Man Singh was a famous robber chief, a sort of Robin Hood figure, known for robbing the rich to give to the poor. Mahārāj jī asked, "Which one is Man Singh?" The brahman said, "That quiet man in his fifties who sits on a blanket, wearing *tulasī* [holy basil wood] beads. He brought you here when he heard reports of your discourse at the Hanumān temple. We are all sepoys of the rāja, that is why the guns. But there is no question of your own security. Your safety is assured."

On the last day of the discourse, there was a huge feast for villagers from miles around. Thousands came, all day long. Mahārāj jī ate nothing, and every gift that was offered to him he gave away.

The next day Mahārāj jī and Śarma were given four horses and told, "These horses will lead you to the road at the edge of our kingdom. When they stop, you get off, and they will return to the village." So Mahārāj jī rode on one horse, Śarma on another, and the *Bhāgavata Purāṇa* and their baggage on the other two. When the horses stopped at a road, they got down, having no idea where they were. The road was deserted, but after a long time, at dusk, a bus came along. It was not going to stop, as this was bandits' territory, but Mahārāj jī threw himself in front of it. The driver stopped and asked where he was going. Mahārāj jī asked where the bus was going; he, of course, would go anywhere. (Śarma, meanwhile, was desperately trying to climb on, and the frightened passengers were trying just as hard to keep him off.) "Agra," said the driver. Greatly relieved, Majārāj jī climbed aboard—fortunately, the bus driver was convinced of his honesty—and they rode to Agra and then home.

The form of discourse Mahārāj jī delivered to Hanumān and then to Man Singh was the *saptāha kathā*, a seven-day series of discourses on the *Bhāgavata Purāṇa*. These customarily last two and a half to three hours at a time, twice a day. They are generally sponsored by businessmen as acts of religious devotion and as a means of supporting—and listening to—a guru to whom they look for guidance. The daytime kathās tend, naturally, to be attended chiefly by women and retired men, but the evening ones are attended by younger men as well. Mahārāj jī was much sought after to give these discourses because he spoke in ordinary language and was talented in dramatizing the stories he used as the basis of his homilies. In following his vocation, Mahārāj jī was above all energetic in drawing on and reinvigorating traditional forms of preaching. Like all successful preachers, he applied the message of the texts to the problems of his listeners in a vivid way; in addition, he had a good singing voice and was especially gifted at using song and poetry to enliven his discourses. Using snatches of song and poetry to punctuate a discourse was a traditional technique, but Mahārāj jī considerably expanded the musical element in his discourses. This has now become a style used by other preachers as well.

In presenting his message, Mahārāj jī regularly invoked an atmosphere of celebration among his listeners. The *Bhāgavata Purāṇa* declares itself to be an embodiment of Krishna himself, so celebrating the *Bhāgavata* and celebrating Krishna are the same.[3] Celebration could take many forms. One kind of event, for example, involved gathering 108 pandits (108 is an auspicious number) who would chant the entire text together for seven days. Their chanting would take place every morning, and in the evenings Mahārāj jī would lead public meetings on religious and social issues—a traditional form of teaching in which he was highly skilled.

The audiences for Mahārāj jī's discourses varied from a few dozen friends gathered at a private house to an audience of several hundred or even a couple of thousand for the public meetings. Mahārāj jī's growing popularity brought not only listeners but also frequently devotees who took initiation (*dīkṣā*) from him, and most of his long-time devotees were first attracted to him when they heard him speak as a young man. But despite the growing demand for him to speak in public and lend his presence to inaugural and celebratory events, he fiercely defended his belief that teaching the sacred texts (*śāstras*) should be done for neither fame nor profit. To do so, he is fond of saying, is a "failure of talent." His followers feel that in this, as in everything else, he speaks what he believes and acts as he speaks.

To the skeptical outsider, the question of finances is somewhat less clear cut. A brahman cannot, by custom, ask for donations—and yet his supporters must be aware of what is needed. Mahārāj jī is not a wealthy man, and until the 1990s the family lived extremely simply (though in this decade they have built a large new house in Jaisingh Ghera, with an eye to sons approaching marriageable age). Some of his activities are definitely done on a fee-for-service basis, as we shall see. He must pay the bills associated with the celebrations he plans and orchestrates; cooks, decorators, and musicians must be paid, even though their chief motivation is also devotion. The cows that were kept within the ashram until very recently had to be fed—and this cost more than feeding the family and staff. We shall see that although he is not "famous," his wide circle of devotees and friends do support him and enable him to pursue his goals of serving his deity.

Mahārāj jī's beliefs are deeply rooted in his study of the texts and commentaries of the Vaiṣṇava tradition. In addition to the *Bhāgavata Purāṇa*, the texts written by the Six Gosvāmīs under the guidance of Śrī Caitanya Mahāprabhu are the foundation of Caitanyaite teaching.[4] In the 1940s, aware of the need for good editions of the Caitanya literature, Mahārāj jī collaborated with Śrī Purīdāsa Dāsa to edit and publish nearly seventy volumes of the Gosvāmīs' works, which remain the standard references for scholars of the tradition. These publications were not only well printed and bound but also so carefully edited and proofread that, it is said, there is not a single printer's error. The books were distributed by him free of cost to libraries and scholars, and sometimes he also bore the shipping costs. Sacred texts, he believes, are not to be sold.

In the mid-1960s, Mahārāj jī became aware that the birthplace of Krishna in Mathura, a few miles from Vrindaban, was a neglected, dilapidated site. The temple that once stood there had been destroyed by Aurangzeb's forces, and only a platform remained, with an underground cell. Mahārāj jī had the cell excavated and began going there himself every morning at 6:00, driving himself in a car; there, each day, he read the chapter in the *Bhāgavata Purāṇa* describing Krishna's birth (X.3) and gave a discourse on the subject. Local people, including dignitaries, began attending, and soon a movement was afoot to restore the site. In 1968, Mahārāj jī joined Hanuman Prasad Podar, the legendary editor of the Gita Press (which publishes the *Bhāgavata Purāṇa* and other texts for sale very cheaply), in laying the cornerstone for the main temple now there.

Mahārāj jī's musical inclinations led him to work intensively with the form of theater called *rāsalīlā*. Rāsalīlās, as we have seen, were first presented outside the temples of Vrindaban in the eighteenth century, in Jaisingh Ghera. These musical dramas combine a prologue of poetic celebration of Krishna, enlivened by sedate dancing, with a dramatized episode from one of the stories from Krishna's childhood.[5] They may be performed at any time but are especially current during the six weeks of the monsoon. This is the season of the annual pilgrimage around Vraja, the *vana yātrā* (which Caitanyaite Vaiṣṇavas do in three weeks; others may take more or less time), when all the sites of Krishna's līlās are visited. At many of the sites a rāsalīlā is staged, so the pilgrims can see and experience the līlās more fully.[6] A cycle of rāsalīlās is also performed at Jaisingh Ghera for six weeks during the monsoon season. Over the years, Mahārāj jī has worked with various rāsalīlā troupes to improve their performances, guiding the performers through both the literature and the techniques, and always innovating.

In the 1940s, collaborating with Bābā Premānanda, he started a variation on this theatrical form called the Caitanya līlā or Gaurāṇga līlā. Here the stories presented in the second half, though structured like the Krishna rāsalīlās, are from Caitanya's life. Although there was a tradition in Bengal of dramatic recitations of stories from the life of Caitanya, the Goswamis believe this was the first time his life was enacted in Braj bhāṣā, the major regional dialect of Hindi. In 1983, Mahārāj jī took the rāsalīlā troupe he had been working with on a grand tour of Western Europe for the first time. He again led the troupe to France for the Festival of India in 1986.

The other major dramatic innovation of Mahārāj jī was the aṣṭayāma līlā. For each of the aṣṭayāma līlās (twenty-four hours or more of stage time), Mahārāj jī writes the script, chooses music, oversees the creation of sets and costumes, and selects and trains the performers. In 1989, a day in the life of Caitanya was presented as equivalent to a day in the life of Krishna, and in 1992 and 1996 aṣṭayāma līlās of Krishna himself were staged.

Over the years, Mahārāj jī became increasingly involved on the managing committees of various religious and educational institutions, and in 1972 he founded the Sri Caitanya Prema Samsthana, housed in Jaisingh Ghera, as an umbrella for his own activities in the fields of scholarship, art, music, and drama. In addition to sponsoring rāsalīlās, the Samsthana has supported a revival of the traditional *dhrupada* style of music, which is closely related to the rāsalīlā, through a school and for many years an annual festival. Traditional arts of Vraja—dance, costumes, flower art, and silver crafting, among others—have been supported and encouraged by the Samsthana. An audio and video archive has been established to document these activities, and a library of books and documents on Vraja and the Vaiṣṇava traditions has been assembled. Small groups of Vaiṣṇava scholars regularly gather at Jaisingh Ghera for ongoing study and discussion of sacred texts.

Another field in which Mahārāj jī has considerable expertise is ayurvedic medicine. Traditional medicines are part of every family's stock of knowledge, but Mahārāj jī has carried his study beyond the basics. He studied for a while with an old man in Varanasi, a south Indian *vaidya* (master of ayurvedic medicine). When this man died, Mahārāj jī spent much time with Bābā Pyārī Mohana Dāsa, a retired revolutionary (rumored to have had British blood on his hands) turned vaidya, who lived in Ṭaṭiāsthāna, a peaceful rural area on the south side of Vrindaban that is still home to Vaiṣṇava renunciants of the Haridāsi sect. These days Mahārāj jī continues to collect and prepare his own herbs for a variety of remedies and is known especially for his cure for bloody hemorrhoids.

Mahārāj jī's position as a religious leader was made possible by his birth into the Rādhāramaṇa Gosvāmī lineage, though his own study and attainments were what propelled him into a role of leadership. It is a position that in a similar sense will be inherited by his sons and grandsons. All his children, boys and girls, were educated in Varanasi. His elder son, Shrivatsa, did his undergraduate studies at Banaras Hindu University and continued as a graduate student in philosophy there under the guidance of Professor T. R.V. Murti. Murti was a renowned philosopher, and Mahārāj jī personally asked him to be his son's teaching guru. Shrivatsa became like a member of Murti's family and retains close ties to them.

Although most of the curriculum in philosophy at the university consisted of Western philosophy, Murti declared that his aim was that Shrivatsa should become a first-rate scholar of Vaiṣṇava studies, and he himself read deeply in the field to prepare himself as teacher. Shrivatsa had done much of the work on his dissertation on Jīva Gosvāmī, the one of the Six Gosvāmīs who was most responsible for laying the philosophical foundations of Caitanyaite Vaiṣṇavism, when he left for Harvard to take up a year's fellowship at the Center for the Study of World Religions. On his return, Shrivatsa joined his father in touring the length and breadth of the country and took on other responsibilities at Jaisingh Ghera, and the dissertation was never completed. But Shrivatsa continues his studies, and he lectures and writes frequently for both Indian and international audiences. In 1993, he began giving seven-day *Bhāgavata* discourses. Most of his time, however, is taken up with the management of the ashram, planning and making arrangements for the innumerable rituals, celebrations, and other activities; overseeing the constant building projects within the ashram; counseling devotees, and cultivating the network of supporters, friends, and contacts with whose help the ashram flourishes. He frequently draws on his knowledge of *vāstu śāstra,* the science of building location and arrangement, in advising those who come to him with problems. His special interest is the cause of environmental protection and renewal in Vraja.

Mahārāj jī's younger son, Veṇu Gopāla, after studying Sanskrit, philosophy, and astrology in Varanasi and Pune, went on to study for many years with the renowned musician Pandit Jasraj. He is unmarried and travels extensively with a group of musicians from Vrindaban, giving seven-day discourses that are enhanced with devotional music and song.

Mahārāj jī's sons thus carry on their inherited position, but within the pattern of "being a Gosvāmī" they have developed their own interests and talents. Each has been successful in attracting a circle of supporters, circles that somewhat but not entirely overlap with Mahārāj jī's. Shrivatsa's own two sons have completed college and done graduate work in archaeology and philosophy, respectively, in Pune. They have received initiation in the Rādhāramaṇa temple and have thus entered that lineage, but the way in which they will take up their work, using their individual gifts and opportunities, remains to be seen.

Devotional Practice

Mahārāj jī's primary responsibility is toward his deity, Śrī Rādhāramaṇadeva of Rādhāramaṇa temple. When it is his turn to serve in the temple, the manner in which he performs the service demonstrates his belief that everything in the world belongs to Krishna, and the best should be offered to him. (Mahārāj jī's service in the temple is explored in detail in chapter 5.) But this is only the visible tip of the iceberg of his personal devotional exercises, which begin at four in the morning every day. Prayer, meditation, ritual, and study are at the center of his life, whatever his obligations in the world. *Darśana*—vision—is in Vrindaban considered the reward of participation in worshipful devotion, and there are numerous stories of the visions accorded contemporary and historical holy men.[7] Mahārāj jī had been granted more conventional visions in the past, but the coming of the black bee was clearly a manifestation of a different order.

That he has acquired spiritual power and that this is felt by his devotees is without question. It is not his words alone that attract them to him. He himself explains why the words of one teacher are more effective than those of another: "There is an electric current, a kind of power, that flows from a live body. This power is controlled by yogic powers, and has an effect on other souls-in-bodies. Words that are spoken have no effect on other souls-in-bodies, only what is projected by this power. So even if dharmic [spiritually true] words are spoken, if the actual vibration, the radiations, are adharmic [spiritually untrue], then the effect is adharmic. The character of the speaker can be felt in spite of his words." Mahārāj jī communicates an inner joy—at one level, a sense that he is having fun, but much more deeply that he is at peace with himself and the world. The knowledge—self-knowledge—that permits this joy can be directly communicated, and not just by the power of suggestion. It involves as well the use of a power that he can transmit.

One evening, when I was with Mahārāj jī at a series of discourses he was giving in Puri in Orissa, he was exhausted from several days of intense activity. He was sitting on a veranda with his feet in a tub of hot water, and a few very close devotees were seated around him; one woman was standing behind him, massaging his shoulders. She, too, seemed tired, and I volunteered to take her place. Mahārāj jī indicated that I should join her, and while I was standing behind him, he reached back and put my hand on his head. Unexpectedly and undeniably, an electric current ran through my hand and arm for the several minutes that I remained in contact with him.

A form of devotional practice that brings together many of the elements of Caitanyaite—and Mahārāj jī's—faith is ecstatic chanting of the Lord's name and qualities (*kīrtana*). In the sixteenth century, Caitanya Mahāprabhu and his associates used to gather in the evenings to chant and dance together in praise of Krishna and Rādhā. They also took to the streets in procession, spreading the joy of celebration and their own message of faith. Mahārāj jī, like Caitanya, found in ecstatic chanting a source of devotional strength and joy. In his prime of life, he had seemingly limitless strength as he went on for hours dancing and chanting, playing a drum, and raising his hands in praise of Krishna.

That these sessions generated spiritual power is attested by a story that dates to the mid sixties. At this time, the teenaged daughter of one of Mahārāj jī's early devotees (who had also been a student of Mahārāj jī's teacher in Varanasi) was living in Jaisingh Ghera. She had gone to Rādhāramaṇa temple for the midmorning darśana one day, and then went down to the Yamunā River. She did not appear for lunch, and someone went to look for her; she was found, apparently dead, on the bank of the river. Mahārāj jī was called, and he chanted near her for three hours. Her life returned.[8]

Side by side with Mahārāj jī's devotional practice is his concern for his devotees, with the closest of whom he has a warm friendship. Their love for him is combined, in some, with the conviction that he is an avatar of Caitanya—a saint and a guru—but also a member of their family. On his side, he maintains his responsibility to his own family and the extended family of close devotees, who are also the patrons and supporters who provide for the maintenance of Jaisingh Ghera, the Goswami family, and Sri Caitanya Prema Samsthana (which owns, as a public charitable trust controlled by eleven trustees, all the property and assets of the ashram). Almost without exception, this inner circle of devotees comes from families of successful industrialists and merchants, some from among the top business families of India.

These core devotees generally came to Mahārāj jī through family connections—through parents who knew his father, relatives who went to school with him, or in-laws who had known him from childhood. These families have to some extent used the network of devotees to marry their children to one another and to each others' nephews and cousins and now grandchildren, so the sense of family they feel is not entirely a matter of religious sentiment. They visit Vrindaban at the time of the special occasions celebrated by Mahārāj jī and his family, and in between they are in constant touch by phone, fax, and e-mail. They and their wider families come to Mahārāj jī with business and family problems; he and his elder son, Shrivatsa, advise them with good common sense and the wisdom of the *Bhāgavata Purāṇa*. One of them (or Mahārāj jī's younger son, who is usually away from Vrindaban giving discourses) is present when he can be for their marriages, their house blessings, sometimes their illnesses, and their funerals.

The presence of these core devotees at Jaisingh Ghera is multiplied by a group of somewhat less central but still devoted followers. They also came to Mahārāj jī through family connections or because they heard him give a discourse in their city and were attracted to his learning and simplicity, his spiritual power and evident integrity. To them, as to the core group, Mahārāj jī has given initiation (*dīkṣā*); that is, there has been a mutual, ritual acceptance that he is their guru. Many of these followers help to organize visits and discourses by Mahārāj jī in their cities and they are part of the network that can be called on when there are arrangements to be made in connection with anyone in the extended Goswami family, including other devotees of Mahārāj jī.

Among the visitors to Jaisingh Ghera is a small group of foreign scholars and friends who come to study Vrindaban culture or Vaiṣṇavism, and who use the resources of the audio and video archive, the library, and the network of connections that the Goswamis can make available. The family has always welcomed foreign contact; in the 1990s, three foreigners lived in Jaisingh Ghera on a long-term basis, contributing to the ongoing work of documentation, and serving as hosts and guides for other visitors. They have also become increasingly active in working on the problems of environmental degradation that have struck Vrindaban, like many other places in India, during the last two or three decades.

A still larger circle around Mahārāj jī consists of the many thousands of people who have not necessarily taken initiation from Mahārāj jī but who feel a warmth and admiration for him. Virtually every day, families come to see him—husband and wife, often with children or teenagers or an elderly parent. On weekends, there is a constant stream of such people, day-trippers from Delhi and other nearby areas. They come simply to pay their respects, or because they need his advice on some problem in their lives or his blessing for some undertaking. They are welcomed by Mahārāj jī's daughter-in-law or the young man who is manager of Jaisingh Ghera, depending on who is available and the closeness of the visitors to the family; if at all possible, either Mahārāj jī or one of his sons will spend an hour or two—or three or four—talking with them.

A few years after the appearance of the black bee, Mahārāj jī began to focus his energies in a somewhat different direction. Although he continued to give some discourses on the *Bhāgavata* and remained close to his circle of devotees, he dedicated much of his time to the service of the poorest people of western Orissa, the state in which Caitanya spent most of his adult life. In this work, he followed the example of Gauridāsa, a devotee of Caitanya Mahāprabhu, whom the latter instructed to proselytize the masses of Orissa. At that time, the people in north Bengal and Orissa practiced a religion rooted in the Buddhism that once flourished in the area. (As Shrivatsa Goswami explains, the followers of Caitanya who spread his teachings in Bengal and Orissa expressed their message partly in terms of the elements of this popular Buddhism that were congruent with it, and so Buddhism, in its turn, had a pervasive influence on Caitanyaite Vaiṣṇavism as it developed after its founder's death.) [9] The folk traditions of Caitanya devotionalism remained alive in Orissa despite a lack of religious instruction, and Mahārāj jī undertook to instruct and initiate whole villages. As his activities are described (I have not witnessed them), he sits for hours under the hot sun to bring his teaching to the devout but untutored people who flock to him. Far from supporting him with money or even paying for the modest costs of their initiation—for beads and photographs—many of these people can offer him no more than a handful of rice in exchange, but the joy with which they receive his teaching clearly brings Mahārāj jī strength and vigor.

To these poor villagers, Mahārāj jī offers initiation (*dīkṣā*). This dīkṣā is the same ritual that Mahārāj jī gives to all his wealthier devotees—men, women, and children. The difference in the rituals in Orissa is that in attempting to "bring relief" to thousands, he must initiate fifteen or twenty rather than one, two, or three at a time. Most of these villagers who come to him are young adults; he does not know them individually, but they have heard him speak and want what he has to offer. The wish for dīkṣā is all that is required to receive it.

The initiation consists of three elements. The first is giving a necklace of tulasī beads to each devotee. Tulasī is a variety of basil, a member of the mint family, and sacred to Krishna. There is a well-known story about the inseparability of tulasī and the *śālagrāma* stone, the latter the very embodiment of Krishna (more will be said about śālagrāmas in chapter 5). So whoever wears tulasī around the neck—Caitanyaite Vaiṣṇavas customarily wear a double strand—will never be separated from Krishna.

The second component of initiation is marking the arms, shoulders, and chest with twelve *tilakas*, marks of yellow clay called *gopī candana* (lit., gopīs' sandalwood paste), invoking one of the names of Krishna at each mark. To do this is to invest the parts of the body with a token of the qualities of Krishna (and this is a ritual Mahārāj jī practices for himself after each time he bathes). As the process takes some time—it proceeds one invocation at a time—Mahārāj jī has trained devotees to help him with the initiations in Orissa.

The third component is transmitting the mantras—for the guru, for Krishna, and the mahāmantra ("Haré Krishna, Haré Krishna . . ."). The mantras are to be recited 108 times, the number being counted out on the fingers of the right hand, using each segment of the fingers in a specified order, or counted on a string of tulasī beads held in a small bag on the right hand. Mahārāj jī also gives the initiates a small laminated board with a triptych: pictures of Rādhāramaṇa in the center, Śrī Caitanya on the left, and himself on the right, on which the devotee is to focus while doing his daily devotions. In his first year, Mahārāj jī initiated about two thousand villagers in this way; his motivation is not money or glory—these are hardly forthcoming from such a mission—but to use, as he says, the talents he has been given for the relief of the suffering of mankind.

People suffer, teaches Mahārāj jī, because of the karma they have accumulated in past lives. If nothing is done, they will again be reborn to a miserable existence. But the sacred texts say that one who has taken initiation from a guru is released from this cycle of rebirth in suffering and has the opportunity to achieve bliss, which is the highest aim of humankind. Taking initiation is the first step toward knowledge of one's true self. It establishes a relationship with the guru, which implies more than a personal commitment to a teacher. Theologically, the guru stands in the same relation to Krishna as do the attendants of Rādhā and Krishna (*sakhīs*); he is, as they are, the transformers of divine energy, mediating between humankind and divinity. As such, the guru can guide the devotee to knowledge of Krishna; since Krishna is that which is Real, such knowledge is identical to knowledge of the real Self—which is nondifferent from Krishna. Just as the guru prostrates before Krishna, therefore, the disciple bows down before the guru. The prostration is an expression of accepting a relationship with the transcendent.[10]

Mahārāj jī opens many of his talks with the question, "Who are you?"

"You will tell me 'I am Veena,' " he continues," but I do not want to know your name. I want to know, 'Who are *you*?' You tell me you are a teacher. But I do not want to know what you do; I want to know who you are. You tell me you are an Agrawala from Allahabad. I do not want to know your caste, your city, your nationality. I want to know who *you* are." And he looks around the circle of people gathered to listen.

Someone may answer, somewhat smugly, "I am soul, I am *ātmā*." He still is not satisfied. "How do you know this?" And he goes on with his homily. "When someone dies, what do you say? You say, 'He has gone.' You do not mean his body has gone. You say, 'He has gone.' So who is he? This is proof that he is soul."

And what is soul? The individual ātmā, he says, is a small part of Paramātmā, the eternal Soul of the universe. Just as a cup of water drawn from the ocean is of the same material as the ocean, though it does not have the same power to float a ship, so too the individual soul is of the same substance as the great Soul. And what is that substance? *Ānanda*, bliss. Bliss is identical with Krishna. Awareness of this is what separates human from animal, and it is what gives humans happiness.

This is the recurring theme of Mahārāj jī's talks, to a large group or a small one. Know that you are Soul, Ānanda, God, and serve him in loving devotion; this is the knowledge that frees a person from the weight of the inevitable burdens of life in this world.

This knowledge cannot be absorbed simply by hearing the words. Everyone needs to be in relationship with a teacher to develop spiritually, and the choice of that teacher is very important. The chief quality required of a guru is truth. One of Mahārāj jī's favorite examples of the power of truth is the story of a man who brought his young son to a guru. The boy had been smoking cigarettes, and the father asked the guru to admonish him. The guru listened sympathetically but then asked the father to return with the son after a year. A year passed, and the man and boy came again. The guru spoke to the boy, and immediately the boy was convinced and gave up smoking. Seeing the effectiveness of the guru's admonition, the man asked him why he had waited a full year and had not stopped the boy from this habit immediately. The guru replied that when they came the first time, he himself had the habit of chewing tobacco. Only after giving this habit up for a whole year was he able to speak truly to the boy, and by truth convince him.

According to Mahārāj jī, there are specific qualifications that a guru must possess. The title and image of the guru have been tarnished by individuals in this role who are ambitious, greedy, and licentious, and who seek "fame and profit," as Mahārāj jī angrily remarks. The jaundiced view that many take of some famous gurus is fully justified. But there are many individuals in India who have followed a traditional path of spiritual search and discipline and who have, indeed, an insight into human and divine nature. Having achieved some degree of knowledge of God, having learned in the process of initiation to bow before him, and (in the Rādhāramaṇa Gosvāmī order of the Caitanyaite tradition) being privileged thereby to touch the feet of the deity in the temple, the guru acts as the intermediary, the transformer of divine energy. It is in the context of this tradition that the phrase "guru is god," often heard from the mouths of Hindu preachers, should be understood.

According to Vaiṣṇava teaching, a guru must be born into a family of gurus. He must be a householder, not a renunciant—Mahārāj jī becomes quite heated in denouncing so-called renunciants who have abandoned their family responsibilities but not their quest for followers and donations. The guru must be initiated into service of the deity. And he must have certain spiritual qualities: *satya,* or truth, goodness, and purity; *dayā*, or compassion that extends to all individual souls in all creatures, without differentiation; and *tapas*, conscious self-discipline. He is cultivated in the rigorous spiritual training that is called yoga. Each individual who follows this path has an individual regimen, an individual discipline, under the guidance of a guru. The way of yoga is to control one's desires, keep them within bounds, so that one may have a truer relationship with God. "*Hiṁsā*—violence—is not just striking someone, but more important, thinking inauspicious thoughts, thinking ill, or speaking harshly, and thus spreading adharmic vibrations by thought, speech, and action." The means to achieve *ahiṁsā*—nonviolence—is to develop consciousness that one is a part of God, who is Ānanda, Bliss, and thus share in this universal bliss. The aim, as Mahārāj jī often says in English, quoting Socrates, is to "know thyself."

His devotees see in Mahārāj jī the embodiment of these qualities. A tall, erect man of over seventy, his head shaven, his body wrapped in orange cloth, he walks carefully, steadied by a long walking stick. Mahārāj jī looks serious, notices everything, and admonishes those who have fallen short of his expectations. But when he sees a friend, his face breaks into a smile that seems to envelop his whole being. "We have been waiting for you. Why have you been so long in coming?" His entire attention is on his visitor. His deep voice—authoritative, demanding, a voice of a man whose requests are never directly refused—reflects the enthusiasm that he radiates.

Sādhānikā

This enthusiasm (lit.,"inspiration by God") is communicated in Mahārāj jī's discourses, his chanting, and in the gathering of devotees (*satsang*), to recite the Sanskrit hymns he has chosen for this purpose (in a collection called *sādhanikā*). The sādhanikā has been printed, together with Hindi translations, in small booklets. Each time the group gathers for satsang of this sort, Mahārāj jī begins to speak on a spiritual theme and then leads the responsal chanting from among the texts in the booklet to punctuate his discourse.

In the chant with which Mahārāj jī frequently begins, the Lord, Bhagavān, conveys some very fundamental Hindu religious truths:

1. "You will receive knowledge and experience of my most secret true form, O Brahmā, as well as knowledge of the devotion of pure love, and of striving to attain it.
2. "Only thus, by my grace, can you know truly my extent, and my attributes, my form, my qualities, and my actions.
3. "Before creation, I alone existed. In essence I was neither material nor immaterial, nor could I be understood by means of that pair of opposites. Where nothing created exists, I alone am there; and what appears by means of created forms, I also am there; and I am what remains [when they have disappeared].
4. "That which makes it possible for something inexplicable—with no corresponding reality—to appear in me and obscure my Being, like the shadowy [moon-eating] Rāhu among the stars, should be understood as my māyā.
5. "The bodies of living beings, large or small, created of the five elements, also are permeated by the five great heavenly elements, because these make up the real form of those bodies. The formative causes of those places and forms are those heavenly elements, which are present from the beginning and so cannot be said to enter them; in the same way, from one point of view I enter the bodies of living creatures as their soul, but from the point of view of the soul I cannot enter them because I am already there—there is no object other than my essence.

6. " 'Not this, not this'—from this method of denial—and 'this is, this is'—from this method of relationship—one can realize that the whole substance of Bhagavān's form exists always and everywhere, that this entirety is reality; those who truly desire to know, need only to know this.
7. "By unwavering meditation on this, O Brahmā, you will gain a firm conviction of this final goal; from age to age, you will never be entangled in delusion, though you are the creator of all the various forms."

Śrī Catuḥślokī Bhāgavata[11]

To disentangle the devotional elements in these verses (the adherence to a personalized deity) from the transcendental elements (the adherence to an abstract reality) would be to miss the essential feature of Vaiṣṇava worship. The underlying philosophical principle, formulated by Caitanya's disciples, the Six Gosvāmīs, is "inconceivable difference in nondifference," *acintyabhedābheda.* For Caitanyaites, truth is a matter of "both/and." Krishna is transcendent, but he is also immanent, universal, and multiple.[12] Everything created is and is not illusory, for all creation is real, but it is created by the activity of the illusory power (*māyā*) of the Inconceivable. Our reality—our Self—is a small particle of the Real, which is named Krishna, who is also, and just as really, the playful cowherd boy and the adolescent lover. He—Reality—is not only beyond the senses; he will reveal himself to the devotee who is capable of true, pure, total love.

Much less philosophical, and sung with great gusto by everyone, is a hymn to Krishna in the form of Śrī Jagannātha. Jagannātha is a black, grinning, virtually nonfigurative image of Krishna enshrined in Puri, on the east coast of Orissa, where Caitanya spent his last years. Caitanya is said to have adored Śrī Jagannātha with literally all his being, until one day he merged with the image in the temple and disappeared from this world. As a result, Śrī Jagannātha is regarded with both awe and affection by Caitanyaites. The deity is asked for darśana—seeing.

1. Sometime in the past, absorbed in playing your flute on the banks of the Yamunā in Vrindaban, enjoying the beauty of the faces of the cowherd women like a bee, and worshiped by Lakṣmī, Śiva, Brahmā, Indra, Gaṇeśa, and others—O Lord Jagannātha! Please give me darśana!
2. A flute in your left hand, a peacock feather on your head, yellow silk at your waist, you who attract the sidelong glances of young women always immersed in the playful pastimes of Vrindaban, O Lord Śrī Jagannātha! Come before my eyes!
3. On the banks of the great ocean, in a golden temple atop a beautiful blue mountain, you are seated between your stalwart

> elder brother Balarāma and [your friend] Subhadra. Seated thus, you have granted all the gods the chance to serve you. O Lord Śrī Jagannātha! Come within the range of my vision.

This vision of Krishna the cowherd boy and pastoral deity then becomes melded with a simultaneous awareness of a previous manifestation of Krishna (sometimes expressed as an earlier avatar of Viṣṇu), who killed the tyrant-god Varuṇa. And the goddess of bounty, Lakṣmī, who is said to rest on Krishna's chest in the form of a curl of golden hair (*śrīvatsa*), is mentioned in the same breath as the goddess of wisdom, Sarasvatī, the daughter of the god Brahmā.

4. O Ocean of Compassion, destroyer of Varuṇa, with dark liquid beauty and smiling lotus face, who dwells amorously with Lakṣmī as well as Sarasvatī, O Lord Jagannātha! Please appear before us, worshiped by the gods and honored with hymns of praise!

Once a year in every Vaiṣṇava temple, the Krishna image is given a ride in a chariot, either around the town or at least around a portion of the temple in the chariot festival (*rathayātrā*). In Puri the chariot is huge, and once a year a vast crowd of devotees gather to see it drawn down the main street by singing, ecstatic devotees—the original juggernaut:

5. At the time of the chariot festival, when you hear the brahmans singing your glory on the road, you are compassionate toward the devotees; you are the friend of the whole world, Lord Jagannātha, Ocean of Compassion. Together with Lakṣmī, daughter of the Ocean, give us darśana.

Next we have a vision of Lord Viṣṇu, asleep between creations of the world. Although Krishna is often said to be an avatar, a manifestation, of Viṣṇu, his devotees consider the reverse to be true. This evocation then shifts seamlessly to merge with the image of Krishna, the lover of Rādhā:

6. Residing in the midst of the blossoming lotus petal at his feet, Bhagavān's feet are borne by the cosmic serpent on his head. Immersed in the bliss of the feeling of Rādhā as well as enjoying Rādhā's company, O Lord Jagannātha, by your grace, please give us darśana.
7. O Lord! I have not entreated you for the glory of kingdoms, jewels, or a mountain of gold, nor have I desired the beautiful damsels desired by all. O Jagannātha, constantly worshiped by Lord Śiva, who was victorious over the God of Desire, what I desire is that you always and continually give me darśana.

8. O Lord Jagannātha, God of gods and vanquisher of this meaningless world, remover of infinite sins, you who are ruler of the Yadavas [the royal lineage of Krishna] and who have compassion toward orphans, please give me darśana.

Śrī Jagannāthāṣṭakam[13]

This complex potpourri of images of the deity is further enriched by another favorite chant, which consists of eight verses in praise of Caitanya Mahāprabhu, the son of Śacī. Caitanya was not merely a great saint; he is regarded as the manifestation of Krishna and Rādhā in one body:

1. He has taken birth in a beautiful fair body with a golden luster, and always gives the world the enjoyment of feeling, the beloved son of Śacī—by just a fragment of his grace the world is purified. I pay homage to him.

Caitanya was known above all for his ecstatic chanting (*kīrtana*), sometimes in the courtyard of a disciple's house, sometimes in noisy processions through the streets, surrounded by his disciples, for hours on end. This activity aroused the hostility of the more sober residents, the traditional brahmans, but also overwhelmed, disarmed, and even converted villains who wished to harm him or his disciples:

2. The lofty sound of his holy chanting, rising from a heart pounding with the feeling of overflowing love, made the villain afraid—but by his grace, the world's fear was dispelled. I pay homage to this beloved son of Śacī.

Then Caitanya is praised in terms that are conventionally used to describe Krishna:

3. Wearing ocher clothes, with beautiful cheeks, Śrī Śacī's beloved son has nails so beautiful they make even the moon ashamed, so that it sings joyful praise of the name and virtues of the Lord. To him I pay homage.

And then he is spoken of as a gopī (cowherd girl) whom Krishna has abandoned:

4. The stream of tears of separation flow from his lotus eyes—he who is adorned with all the emotions of a loving devotee as he dances slowly, the son of Śrī Śacī. To him I pay homage.
5. He who dances the holy chants with a restless step, wears entrancing, radiant bells on both his ankles; his lotus face is cooler than the moon's. I pay homage to the beloved son of Śacī.

One of the traditional images of Caitanya is then evoked—he carries a staff and mendicant's water pot. This iconography is melded with that of Krishna in the verses that follow:

6. A sacred thread over his shoulder, a staff and water pot in his hand, his head bent, with a divine body, Śrī Śacī's beloved son has banished the sins of the wicked with the staff he carries. To him I pay homage.
7. His locks of hair dust-covered, his red lips sweetly entrancing, adorned with a bright sandalwood mark on his forehead—I pay homage to the beloved son of Śrī Śacī.
8. His beautiful eyes like the soft leaves of lotus, his heavenly body with long, beautiful arms, dressed as a dancer—to Śrī Śacī's son I pay homage.

Śrī Śacītanayāṣṭakam

Another beautiful hymn, set to a very haunting melody, was written by a great follower of Caitanya Mahāprabhu, Jīva Gosvāmī, in praise of the divine couple. It plays on the inseparability of Rādhā and Krishna, each essential to the other, the two complementary aspects of divine truth.

1. For Krishna, Rādhā is love embodied; for Rādhā, Krishna is love made real.
   While I live and when I die, Rādhā-Krishna is my destiny.
2. Rādhā's treasure trove is Krishna, Krishna's treasure trove is Rādhā.
   While I live and when I die, Rādhā-Krishna is my destiny.
3. Rādhā is his breath of life, Krishna is her living breath.
   While I live and when I die, Rādhā-Krishna is my destiny.
4. The joy of Krishna's being fills her to the brim, he is drowning in the joy of Rādhā's being.
   While I live and when I die, Rādhā-Krishna is my destiny.
5. Krishna lives in Rādhā's heart, she's the pleasure of Krishna's heart.
   While I live and when I die, Rādhā-Krishna is my destiny.
6. In Krishna's consciousness stays Rādhā, in Rādhā's consciousness he's fixed.
   While I live and when I die, Rādhā-Krishna is my destiny.
7. Rādhikā is dressed in blue, Śrī Krishna's decked in yellow silk.
   While I live and when I die, Rādhā-Krishna is my destiny.
8. Vṛndāvana's empress—Rādhikā, Vṛndāvana's master—Śrī Krishna.
   While I live and when I die, Rādhā-Krishna is my destiny.

Śrī Śrījīvagosvāmīpāda Viracita Śrīyugalāṣṭakam

Mahārāj jī ends his satsang with a prayer spoken by the devotees following him in unison:

> O Lord! May the world prosper; may there be a clear understanding of the good; may there be mutual goodwill among all living beings; may everyone consider the welfare of one another; may our minds and hearts be inclined toward the path of happiness, and from an emotion of disinterested wisdom may we all seek Śrī Hari [Krishna].

This is a path he has always sought to follow, and along which he has tried to show the way to his friends and family.

The path Mahārāj jī has taken cannot be neatly labeled as that of either householder or renouncer—he is both: *acintyabhedābheda*, indescribable difference in nondifference. Although categories of spiritual discipline are useful analytical tools, they are not pigeonholes within which individuals can be placed. They are more like diagnostic symptoms that can be manifested in various combinations. Personal vows that are taken must be observed with utmost seriousness, but the nature of these vows is variable within a wide range, and each individual finds a particular balance between worldly responsibilities and individual search and devotion. The balance Mahārāj jī has found involves, for instance, keeping in close touch with his family by phone when he is traveling—in no sense renouncing them or abdicating his sense of responsibility—but it has not included spending a lot of time at home. (This made his vow to spend an entire year in Vrindaban after the appearance of the black bee especially noteworthy. The day after his year was up, calculated by the lunar calendar, he was on a plane to Calcutta.)

An important part of Mahārāj jī's teaching concerns the relative importance of family in one's life. Family attachments and concerns, he says, tie up most of people's attention. This is because of the false belief that one's body, and the bodies of one's family, are related to one's self. Meanwhile, although people may give service to the deity with reverence and respect, their thoughts and concerns for family members distract them from performing this service with utmost devotion. These relationships should be reversed. One should treat one's family members with respect, serve them with courtesy, and not show anger; but one should save one's deepest love for that with which one has a real and permanent relationship—ātmā, the self, which one truly is. The physical body and its relations are only temporary.

Further, if one continues to be occupied primarily with relations of the body, one is giving up the truly exceptional opportunities afforded by human birth. Even the gods, who in their exalted state are using up their acquired good karma, do not have the opportunity that humans have to gain the knowledge that allows them to approach Bhagavān, God. The entire purpose of human birth is to remember one's real relationship with God, even while taking care of the family properly. Whatever the difficulties, one must not give up, but remember that although the physical body's relationships end with death, the ātmā's relationships do not. One's eternal relationship is with God.

THREE

THE WOMEN OF THE FAMILY

The family is the context within which the one-to-one relationship of individual and deity is nurtured in Hindu society. This spiritual life depends centrally on the adult women, who marry into the patrilocal family; in Mahārāj jī's family, there have been one, two, or three generations of women present at any given time (Figure 5). They work hard and are dedicated to care of the family as their spiritual discipline. Much of their time, in addition to that spent performing and overseeing the daily work of the household, is given over to private devotions or in preparations for the larger rituals that fill the annual calendar. They also have primary responsibility for welcoming and providing for the many visitors who come to the guru's ashram.

The center of Mahārāj jī's family was his mother as long as she lived; when she died, his wife played this role. As his wife grew older, his daughter-in-law, Shrivatsa's wife, Sandhyā, assumed more and more of the responsibility. Because Mahārāj jī was often gone for as long as three months at a time, giving discourses and visiting his devotees, and his adult sons have likewise traveled a lot, many of the household decisions, even major ones, have been made by the women, although Mahārāj jī has always kept in close touch by telephone.

Before 1965, the family lived in a two-story house with a walled garden in Rādhāramaṇa Gherā, just a few yards from the entrance to Rādhāramaṇa temple. In 1962, Mahārāj jī gained possession of Jaisingh Ghera, but there was no usable living space there, and it was not used by the family until 1965, when a guest house was built to house the visitors

Figure 5. The Goswami family, 1992. Left to right: Sandhyā, family friend, Shrivatsa, Mātā jī, Rājū (behind), Mahārāj jī, Sonī.

for Mahārāj jī's eldest daughter's wedding. The guest house was one story high, built around an open courtyard. After the wedding, Mahārāj jī's wife—who had overseen its construction—decided it would be more comfortable to live there than in the old house, and the family moved. The house in Rādhāramaṇa Gherā thereafter served, in turn, as a guest house for long-term visitors.

The responsibilities of the women in a guru's family center on several functions: raising the children, maintaining hospitality, assisting with preparations for the rituals and celebrations conducted by the family, generally keeping the house going, and above all pursuing their own spiritual lives. The devotions of the guru's wife, like those of all family members, are carried on within the household, although she also makes regular visits to Rādhāramaṇa temple and, on special occasions to, other temples in Vrindaban. She is responsible for maintaining the family *sevā*—

service of the household deity—which, together with her individual devotions, can take several hours each day.

Mahārāj jī's mother was the acknowledged leader of women's devotional singing in the neighborhood, and especially on the eleventh day of every lunar fortnight (*ekādaśī,* a day marked for special devotion) she would call to her neighbors to come join in a session of chanting the names and qualities of the Lord (*kīrtana*)—not the ecstatic dancing of Mahārāj jī and the men around him, but a quiet circle of women. She played the harmonium, another woman played the rhythms on a drum, while others clapped little hand cymbals, and all sang from the vast repertoire of songs in the Vraja tradition—songs of longing, of loneliness, of joy in the love of Rādhā and Krishna, songs of seasonal festivals as they came and went. The custom has been maintained by the wives of her son and grandson, whenever there are enough women in the house to participate and time can be spared. It is an extension of the time of individual worship for each of the women, but it is also a time for them to enjoy one another's company while they renew their inner equilibrium and dedication to the deity they serve through their daily hard work.

Mahārāj jī's mother is remembered by her grandchildren as a strong woman, very loving, jolly, and fun-loving, who maintained a devout and peaceful household. It is said that everything in her household was done properly and aesthetically, as tradition and ritual required. And the house was always open to visitors. In the Rādhāramaṇa house, Mahārāj jī's mother lived in one room, he and his wife and children—there were five children in all, though rarely were they all there at one time—in another room. The other rooms in the house were for visitors. Because of the atmosphere, the grandchildren remember that, entering that place, "you knew you were coming into a guru's house."

Besides the activities of ritual and individual worship, the dominant household activity is another manifestation of devotion—the preparation and serving of food. All food to be eaten by members of the Goswami family is offered first to the deity in the household shrine. Food cooked in the separate kitchen that nowadays serves staff and visitors is first offered to a picture of Rādhāramaṇa, then to Hanumān, whose shrine is in the garden of Jaisingh Ghera and who will himself accept only food that has already been offered to Krishna. After the deity has partaken, the "leftovers" (*praśāda*) are served.

The diet of the family is subject to numerous rules of ritual purity, but most fundamentally it is strictly vegetarian and forbids even garlic, onion, and mushrooms. Mahārāj jī, however, places no dietary restrictions as a condition of taking initiation (*dīkṣā*). But, he says, the devotee should be aware that it is not his body that is eating—the body by itself is "like a stick" and has no ability to take any action. It is the soul that has life, and that eats—and what one eats affects the soul.[1] In effect, the diet becomes closely regulated for those who are able to choose what they eat. (The impoverished Orissan farmers, for example, have little choice, but Mahārāj jī claims that some 85 per cent of those who have taken initiation from him have become vegetarian and have given up alcohol.)

In addition, each member of the family and each devotee chooses among the traditional cycles of fasting—once or twice a week, on the eleventh day of the lunar half-cycle, and on special days of observance. Fasting may be complete, may mean fruit and liquid, or may mean special, deliciously prepared foods that exclude grains. It is entirely up to each person what to do in this respect.

Preparation of the food is thus primarily a service to the deity—and to the soul which is a part of the deity. The primary requirement of a cook in the Goswami household is love of and devotion to Krishna. But care is just as important as love, and thus there are strict rules that govern the preparation. The cook must be ritually pure, having participated in no "unclean" activities since taking a bath. If the food is being prepared for Mahārāj jī, the cook should wear silk. And if the cook is a woman, she is excused for the first four days of her menstrual period, for at this time she is ritually impure. (Not only can she not cook but also she cannot touch anyone else in the household or come in contact with anything made of cloth that others will handle, such as rugs or chair cushions. Needless to say, she cannot enter the temple.) And servants are human; in the mid-1990s, one old woman still claimed this monthly rest even though she was obviously well past menopause: who was to challenge her claim of impurity?

Some types of food are more susceptible to ritual contamination than others; least susceptible are fried foods, which are therefore considered safest and most pleasing. And the threat of contamination is ever present. Food may not be tasted, even to check for flavor, before it is offered to the deity, for humans may eat the deity's leftovers, but not vice versa—nor may humans eat food from a plate another has eaten from.

Because food is served not only at mealtime but also whenever any of the members of the family ask for it and whenever visitors arrive, food preparation is a major occupation of the women and household staff of the Goswami household. Grains and beans have to be sifted to pick out the stones, vegetables cut up, and spices ground each day. Often helping with these tasks are three or four older women, widows, who live elsewhere but who have been associated with the family for years, and who may come for weeks or months at a time to stay and participate in the life of the ashram.

Another household task, sewing, is minimal for household needs, because both men and women wear primarily unsewn clothing—saris, dhotis, and shawls. But periodically, sewing becomes a major activity, as preparations are made for the performances of the rāsalīlā performances, which take place for six weeks during the monsoon and again for four days in the spring, during Holī. Although many of the costumes are reused from one performance to another, there are always some new ones to be made: for one thing, the actors are mainly children, who grow from year to year. For a major production like the aṣṭayāma līlās, several sets of entirely new clothes are made for the principal actors.

The costumes are all made in Jaisingh Ghera. They are designed by the women—these days, Shrivatsa's wife—consulting with Shrivatsa and Mahārāj jī, and they shop for the shimmering silks and the gold and silver thread embellishments. If there are many costumes to be made, a tailor is hired to come and sit on a veranda, stitching the skirts and blouses, shirts and coats; a talented servant in the ashram also stitches many of them. All the trimming with gold and silver borders, filigree rosettes, teardrops, and stars is done by hand by women in the household. The work goes on day in and day out for weeks or months before the performance, and into the night under the dim lightbulbs (usually dim in the evening because of electrical "load shedding"). The rest of the household activities take place while the sewing continues, including offering hospitality to the visiting women who come and go in their guru's household.

As Mahārāj jī's mother grew older, she said her chief wish was that she might die in her son's arms, but that this would be impossible because he traveled thirteen months out of every twelve. But in 1972, when she was sixty-seven, on one ekādaśī she bathed and came out saying she did not feel well. Mahārāj jī took her in his lap and held her, chanting verses from the *Bhāgavata Purāṇa* for half an hour, and then she just died.

Mahārāj jī's wife then became the matriarch of the household and began to be respectfully called Mātā jī, "Mother," although those close to her continued to call her Jījī, "Elder Sister." She came from a prominent traditional priestly family in Mathura; she had a high school education, and Mahārāj jī encouraged her to continue her studies and to graduate from college after marriage, despite open opposition from more orthodox Gosvāmīs. Mātā jī's mother, who had died when Mātā jī was six or seven years old, came from an aristocratic family, whose men were gurus to "nobility." She dressed perfectly and left her beautiful daughter with a firmly established sense of elegance and of doing things properly. Despite her education and accomplishments, Mātā jī maintained quite strict seclusion in the home. She would go to Rādhāramaṇa temple with other household women; it was across the courtyard for many years, and even after the family moved to Jaisingh Ghera, it was a short walk down a narrow alley behind the compound. On special occasions, she would go to other temples in Vrindaban, and she loved to travel with Mahārāj jī when she could. But she would certainly never walk down to the bazaar to go shopping, for example; such was a job for a servant.

The travels that Mātā jī shared with Mahārāj jī were usually visits to devotees for weddings or on the occasion of seven-day discourses. A more special occasion for travel was the occasional pilgrimage (*yātrā*) that Mahārāj jī led to sacred sites in the four corners of India: Puri, Rāmeśvaram, Dvārakā, and Badrīnātha. The temples at these far-flung sites are goals for all Vaiṣṇava pilgrims; since about two hundred devotees accompany Mahārāj jī on these trips, they are major undertakings. Mahārāj jī and his family make all the arrangements—travel, lodging, food—with the help of a few devotees who give their time to this very complex operation.

The central event in most of the journeys is a seven-day *Bhāgavata* discourse by Mahārāj jī or, recently, by Shrivatsa at the destination. This means, for instance, that the sound system must be brought on the train or bus or however the group is traveling, as well as materials for decorating the platform on which the speaker is to sit. Pūjās are performed morning and evening, and the materials for these must be carried along. Meals must be arranged along the way and at the destination. Lodging—accommodating a wide range of individual needs, budgets, and preferences—must be arranged. The Goswami women are an important part of the planning operation, and in preparing whatever must be brought. But those who have traveled in India know that, even with thorough planning, things do not work out as expected. Each step is improvisational theater—an itinerary is established, props are provided, all is arranged for as well as possible—and then the play begins.

The trip itself has a holiday air, though the focus is always devotion to Krishna. In Puri, for example, in addition to the discourse several hours each day in a pavilion near the main temple of Jagannātha, there were visits to the temple and to places associated with Caitanya's many years spent in Puri. Mahārāj jī spoke at each place and led his followers in singing or chanting sādhānikā hymns and, on occasion,

Figure 6. Mahārāj jī doing kīrtana in Puri, 1991.

kīrtana (Figure 6). In Dvārakā, in addition to discourses by Shrivatsa in a pavilion within the temple compound, there was an expedition by boat to Bait Dvārakā, an island off the shore associated with what is believed to be Krishna's sunken capital city (Figure 7), and there were visits to one of Mīrā Bāī's temples on the journey there and to the long-contested site of Somnātha on the way home. These outings are enjoyed by all, but perhaps by the women even more than the men, because their daily lives are more constrained.

As a young woman in the household at Rādhāramaṇa Gherā, Mahārāj jī's wife was strong in both body and opinion. The household was run with very little help from servants; she used to carry all the water for household use from the well in the courtyard of the house—thirty or forty buckets a day. She not only cared for the children but also helped look after for the many visitors who were always around.

All her life, Mātā jī personally cooked all Mahārāj jī's food—assisted, in her later years, by her daughter-in-law or a brahman woman servant. After her mother-in-law's death, she continued to run the household strictly, insisting that the traditional ways be maintained. Her contribution to important decisions was enhanced by her ability to draw up horoscopes, an ability she passed on to her younger son.

As Mātā jī grew older, the physical tasks in the household were increasingly taken over by her daughter-in-law, Sandhyā. Sandhyā is highly educated in Sanskrit and Hindi, the eldest of eight sisters in a prominent Vrindaban family who were raised to value the rich tradition of Vaiṣṇava literature. Though after she married she lived with her husband and their small children first in Varanasi and then in Cambridge, Massachusetts, while he was studying, once she settled in Jaisingh Ghera, she too was subject to strict rules. Her chief outlet was the study of singing, in which she became quite accomplished; she also wrote songs that were added to the repertoire sung in the women's kīrtanas. When, in 1993, Shrivatsa began giving seven-day discourses, she broke new ground for Goswāmī women by appearing beside him and singing the songs that punctuate and enrich these discourses.

Although Mātā jī suffered from arthritis in her later years, she remained the central pillar of the household until her death in 1995. She usually sat in her armchair in the courtyard of the family house, out of the sun and within arm's reach of the phone. She practically never went out, but many people came to her; she was always there for children or grandchildren, cousins or friends—anyone who wanted to talk. It was to her that the young people felt they were returning home on visits. Many of the women devotees came especially to see her. She would welcome them and sit with them for hours while talking, counseling, gossiping. There was almost always a small knot of people gathered around her. In the evenings, in the years before her death, she sat in front of the television set, remote control in hand; other members of the household, occasionally including Mahārāj jī, would join her. All important decisions were made only after consulting her, and her opinions on many matters were said to have overruled Mahārāj jī's.

Mātā jī had a rich sense of humor. I remember particularly the occasion of a "birthday party" for Shrivatsa. When Shrivatsa and Sandhyā had returned from a year in the United States, Sandhyā suggested to Mahārāj jī that family birthdays be observed, as they are in the West. He

Figure 7. Mahārāj jī doing kīrtana in Bait Dvāraka, 1994. Photo by Robyn Beeche.

agreed, and these celebrations were added to the already crowded calendar of ritual observances. A birthday was calculated by the lunar calendar—such-and-such a day of the bright (or dark) half of such-and-such a month—and full observances were held for the birthdays of Mahārāj jī's sons and grandsons, if they were in Vrindaban. (I never observed any celebration of birthdays of women of the household.)

For twenty-four hours, groups of Vaiṣṇava kīrtana singers would sing or chant the auspicious name of the Lord continually, in three- or four-hour relays, somewhere in the public space of Jaisingh Ghera. These Vaiṣṇavas are men who are not full renunciants (*sannyāsīs*)—Caitanya forbade vows of full renunciation among his followers—but they are not ordinary householders, either. They are celibate devotees who live in small groups, often with a guru, pursuing their devotional exercises; others call them *viraktas* or simply Vaiṣṇavas. These particular Vaiṣṇavas make their living by chanting kīrtanas at ritual events; they are regularly called to Jaisingh Ghera to play and chant for twenty-four or forty-eight hours on special occasions, though they may come for shorter sessions as well. The sound of the drums and the chanting, which can be heard throughout the ashram day and night, creates an insistent reminder that besides the occupations and preoccupations of ordinary life there is a call to awareness of another life.

On the morning of the birthday, a pūjā was conducted by the family priest in front of the tulasī plant that was kept in the center of the courtyard of the family house. The kīrtana singers provided background music. One year someone brought the family a yellow plastic daisy in a flower pot, which moved in time to nearby sounds, such as music. Mātā jī had the flower brought and set in front of the Vaiṣṇavas, and she laughed harder than anyone else at the look on the faces of the astonished singers.

Like her father-in-law and her mother-in-law, Mātā jī died suddenly and peacefully. The irony was that she was not at home in Vrindaban, and no member of her family was with her. She had gone to Mumbai to attend a seven-day *Bhāgavata* discourse of Mahārāj jī at the home of one of his devotees. She had traveled there partly because she wanted to consult doctors in Mumbai for her arthritis. Most of the rest of the family had also gathered—a somewhat unusual occurrence—as their personal schedules allowed, to be present and listen to the discourse.

Mahārāj jī's major theme in this particular discourse was to emphasize again and again that a person is not the body that dies but the soul that lives on. He talked about how to prepare for the separation of the two, and he went through the cycle of Krishna līlās that are normally observed in the course of a seven-day discourse only perfunctorily. Later, he was said to have been prescient. Mātā jī listened to the whole discourse, two and a half to three hours every morning and evening for a week. Then the family went their separate ways to other obligations, and she stayed to consult the doctors. One evening she complained of chest pains and was nauseous. A doctor was called, gave her an electrocardigram, and said it was normal, but she was uneasy all night. The doctor was again called in the morning; he took her blood pressure and said she was fine. She had a bath, tried to eat some porridge, and then quite simply and quietly she lay back and stopped breathing, her face peacefully composed. Friends were with her at the end, but no family.

Mahārāj jī, who was by now in Calcutta, and the rest of the family, who were in Delhi, Varanasi, and Vrindaban, were called. One daughter who lived in Mumbai came immediately and joined the weeping friends. Mahārāj jī talked on the phone several times with the mourners, telling them that there was no cause for grief, that although her body remained, her real self had joined the Real—Ānanda, Bliss. Nevertheless, the men wept and the women wailed without reserve.[2]

At first, it was thought that she would be cremated in Mumbai and her ashes taken to Vrindaban, but it was finally decided that her body would be embalmed and taken to Vrindaban to be cremated on the banks of the Yamunā. A body should normally be burnt before the sun has crossed the horizon twice after death, but in this case, it was considered more important that the cremation be in Vrindaban than that the time constraints be observed.

Within an hour, Mātā jī's body had been removed from the bed, and the bed itself was dismantled and removed, with all the bedding, from the apartment. It was polluted by death and had to be destroyed. The body was laid on a mat on the stone floor, which had been lightly smeared with ritually purifying cow dung paste, her feet to the south. (It is considered inauspicious for any but the dead and dying to lie in this direction of Yama, the god of death.) Small pieces of cotton were placed in her nostrils. As people arrived, they sat with her or talked together in the living room and dining room.

Members of the immediate family arrived in the evening. Shrivatsa sat with Mātā jī, reading the *Bhagavad Gītā* to her. He interrupted the reading only to make phone calls to arrange to have her body carried that night on a flight to Delhi. It went in a casket bedecked with garlands, in the cargo hold, and when it came off the plane, I was told, every garland was still in place. From the airport, it was carried to Jaisingh Ghera, where it was placed in the room off the main rāsalīlā hall. After some time, she was dressed in a beautiful red and gold sari and placed on a ritually prepared bamboo stretcher; flower petals and garlands were placed over her and at her head and feet, and coconuts at her feet. In the afternoon, she was carried by her sons, sons-in-law, and friends through the town to the burning ground on the banks of the Yamunā River. Formal notice of a death is not sent out for three days, but word spread quickly through the town, and a large crowd gathered to follow the procession. Normally women must stay at home when the body leaves, but in this case women devotees (not family members) also came to the riverbank for a final farewell; they had to leave before the fire was lit.

On the way to the burning ground, water from the Yamunā was poured on the ground in her path. The sacred dust of Vrindaban was sprinkled on her face, and it was reported that at that moment the color of her face turned from blue to golden. Once at the burning ground, the body was dipped in the Yamunā before being placed on the pyre. Her younger son, Veṇu Gopāla, placed her hands under her body so they would not fly out as the body was consumed. Shrivatsa, as the chief mourner, had his head shaved beside the river, and at dusk, when all members of the family had been able to come and pay their last respects, he lit the pyre. After two hours, he crushed the skull with a long staff and poured in ghi from a coconut cup at the end of a pole. As the pyre burned lower and lower, I was told, there was a sense that the separation of body and soul had gone peacefully, that ashes and dust were returning to dust.

The cremation took place on the second day of the thirteen-day mourning period. There were certain customs and rituals to be performed during each of the remaining days. It was a sign of Mahārāj jī's great respect for and devotion to his wife that there was an unusually full observance of the mourning period.

Members of the immediate family could not do any "business as usual" in this period, and Shrivatsa took a personal vow not to speak on the phone or write any letters in this time. Any food eaten by the mourners had first to be ritually offered to the cows in the cowshed of Jaisingh Ghera and then to the deity, and once a day a portion was eaten by Shrivatsa (his only meal of the day); only then was food served to others. In addition, Shrivatsa ritually served a meal to a selected brahman each day. Neither he nor any of the closely related male relatives could shave for ten days. Throughout the period, groups of Vaiṣṇavas chanted kīrtanas in the hall or in one of the rooms just off it.

Death notices are supposed to be sent—and the first visitors offering condolences received from outside—on the third day of the mourning period, but this was a Thursday. Tuesdays, Thursdays, and Saturdays are to be avoided for all ritual occasions as inauspicious days. So the third day was a quiet one, during which the family and close friends stayed and talked in the courtyard of the house, remembering Mātā jī. People feel that by talking about the deceased, their memory will be established and confirmed in those who remain behind. Shrivatsa and Mahārāj jī stationed themselves at the end of the performance hall and began to make the further arrangements, and Mahārāj jī talked with whoever came to him about the nature of self and soul; he told them that the body is something that is left behind when the true self—the soul—departs.

It was on the fourth day that notices were printed and addressed; in the afternoon of that day, large straw mats were spread in the hall, and in mid-afternoon people started arriving to give their condolences. The men gathered in the great hall, the women in the smaller hall behind. Meanwhile, the family was beginning to prepare for the rituals of the twelfth day, when a final goodbye would be said to Mātā jī. Lists were being made, and the men and boys started going out to do the shopping: a collection of all the things Mātā jī used in her daily life, but brand new, were to be given away to the wife of the family priest, who on the final day acted as a proxy for the departing person.

As a focus for the mourners, a photograph of Mātā jī was framed and placed on a table facing the main door of the hall, with a tulasī plant and some garlands. Another photo was placed in her chair in the house, and a third in the room where she had lain before cremation. Her absence was being bridged over as gently as possible. Every morning a different *Bhāgavata* scholar-preacher came and gave a discourse for the departed soul.

In the late afternoon of the sixth day, a group from Navadvīpa in Bengal—Caitanya's birthplace and a center of Caitanyaite Vaiṣṇavism—arrived and began narrating and enacting stories from the life of Caitanya. The main performer, standing not on the stage but in the middle of the hall near Mātā jī's picture, sang and narrated the stories and acted them as well, with a young drummer as an occasional foil. A violinist, harmonium player, cymbalist, and flute player provided the sound effects. The performance, all in Bengali, was very vivid and emotional; it lasted two and a half hours. Besides the family, most of those who attended were Bengali widows and renunciants, all in white. It was a very different crowd from the usual colorful, mixed audience for the rāsalīlās.

Early in the morning of the seventh day, Mahārāj jī gathered everyone for an hour of satsang, chanting sādhānikā hymns. For the remainder of the mourning period, this was to be a most important activity for family and friends. The Navadvīpa group performed again each day, and there was satsang twice a day. Each day the group gathering for satsang grew; on the eighth day, it was joined by the leader of the rāsalīlā group sponsored by the Goswamis. After the evening satsang, he and some others gave a "concert"—but it was performed as a musical offering for Mātā jī, near her portrait rather than on stage.

Some of the major rituals of mourning are traditionally performed on the tenth day, but this fell on a Thursday. So as not to prolong the period of inauspiciousness, these rituals were done on the ninth day. They marked the beginning of the process of cleansing the impurity of death. All the men of the family, including Mahārāj jī's two brothers who live nearby, had their heads shaved, and their beards were shaved for the first time in nine days (one day having been truncated), in a ritual on the riverbank. When the men returned to Jaisingh Ghera, everyone joined in satsang, and emotions flowed over; many of the women, especially, were in tears.

Friends and devotees now began to gather from all over India for the final farewell on the twelfth day, and the audience for the afternoon performance by the Navadvīpa group was about twice the size of that on previous days. People continued to come during the next day, and the previously intimate satsangs became more like congregational groups. In the evening, a performance of classical devotional music was played by local musicians, again in the center of the performance hall, in front of Mātā jī's picture.

The important ritual of feeding the ancestors occurred on the eleventh day, and Shrivatsa's sons—Mātā jī's grandsons—arrived from college for the occasion. Each year, at the end of the monsoons, three deceased generations, both men and women, are ritually fed during a two-week period that is inauspicious for any other ritual. Today, Mātā jī joined this lineage by means of a five-hour worship conducted at Keśighāt by the river (a few hundred yards from Jaisingh Ghera), during which meals were ritually served on leaf plates to the ancestors.

Large numbers of people were now arriving. Because the guest rooms had been filled to capacity and beyond, some of the humbler visitors were beginning to camp out in the common rooms of Jaisingh Ghera. A number of rooms were also engaged outside the ashram; Vrindaban has no public hotel. Mātā jī's picture, now an enlargement in color rather than the black-and-white one that had been displayed earlier, was enshrined on a two-tiered octagonal dais in the main hall, the space around it hung with streamers of fragrant flowers (Figure 8). The afternoon performance by the group from Navadvīpa was followed in the evening by a slide show in the courtyard of the family house. This darśana (as it was specifically called) opened with photographs of Rādhāramaṇa in the gorgeous clothing in which he had been dressed during the Goswamis' service in the temple the previous year, and then moved on to old pictures of Mātā jī and the family. The show was accompanied by a cassette tape of members of the family singing and playing instruments twenty-five years before: the first item in the ashram's audio archive. After this, the famous musician Pandit Jasraj, a longtime friend of

Figure 8. Mātā jī. Photo by Robyn Beeche.

the family who was greatly attached to Mātā jī and who had taught music to her younger son, Veṇu Gopāla, sang in the great hall for four hours in her honor. His performance was one of those rare and special occasions when a great musician sings from his heart to a gathering of close friends and family. Most of the audience, exhausted, left after two or three hours, but a surprising number remained, seated on thin rugs on the marble floor, until 12:30 in the morning, without having had anything to eat since lunch. Then Mahārāj jī called on those who were still there to join in chanting sādhānikā for an hour. Finally at 1:30 the group broke up to eat—the cooks and servants had also waited in the next room, with the dinner—or go to bed, whichever seemed more urgent.

On the twelfth day, there was another pūjā on the ghat. But the climax of the period of saying farewell is the thirteenth day. During the morning, the family and friends were busy gathering together the items needed for three main rituals: first, there was a worship service for the men of the family; second, a ceremony honored thirty-one brahmans with mantras and food and gifts; finally, the priest's wife was sent off with replicas of Mātā jī's worldly possessions.

On the front of the stage, the offerings to the brahmans were arrayed: thirty-one small cloth rugs, each with a large metal plate, a cup, two small metal bowls, a dhoti and a shawl, rubber flip-flop sandals, an umbrella, a sacred thread, a betel nut, a lotus bud, and a small sweet made of sugar and condensed milk (*peḍā*). Nearby, a new folding cot was set up, and on it were placed sheets and pillowcases, quilts and pillows from which the stuffing was falling out—in principle, goods for the deceased are not to be sewn—a gold and red sari, cosmetics and personal items, and a copy of the *Bhāgavata Purāṇa*. Under the cot were a new color television with a remote control, and a new table fan.

The worship service was started by the priests in the room off the main hall where Mātā jī's body had lain, even while things were being gathered in the hall itself for the other two ceremonies. Gradually, male members of the family drifted in to join the proceedings. A fire was built on the marble floor of the small room—making it hot and smoky—and ghi and sesame seeds were put in as mantras were chanted. When the pūjā was finished, the thirty-one brahmans—some of them priests, some friends, some staff of Jaisingh Ghera—were seated in two facing lines on the floor of the large room behind the great hall. The number thirty-one was arrived at by a calculation that condensed into one ritual the year-long ritual obligations of mourning, including the obligation to feed a brahman each day for twelve days, another brahman once a month for six months on the anniversary of Mātā jī's death, and another for twelve months—plus one because the coming year included an intercalary month, inserted in the lunar calendar every three years to keep it in step with the solar calendar. By shortening the period of ritual inauspiciousness, the extended family could get on with happy rituals such as marriages during the coming twelve months. It is not felt that any ritual requirements have been seriously cheated in this way, and, in fact, the monthly feedings are also carried out—a woman (usually the wife of the priest) would be ritually fed one day a month for a year. (If Mātā jī had been a widow, the woman being fed would have been a widow, too.)

While the brahmans ate the feast that had been prepared for them, everyone else squeezed in behind them and chanted the sādhānikā hymns. When the brahmans finished eating, they moved to the big hall and sat in a group at the far end, away from the cot with Mātā jī's things on it, and were handed the small rugs with gift items on them.

Following this, there was a considerable delay while the wife of the priest went into a back room and was dressed by the women and closest friends of the family in the new sari and other items that had been gathered as being Mātā jī's particular, favorite things. Everyone else sat in the hall outside, silent or talking in low voices. When she came out, the priest's wife sat on the cot while everyone filed past to touch her feet and pay their last respects. Several were weeping. When everyone had had a turn, she was escorted out of the hall to a waiting car, into which all the material goods associated with Mātā jī were piled. As she rode away, the final farewell was said. The rest of the mourners lined up in rows in the great hall, to be served the funeral feast. Those who served the guests were the family members and closest devotees of Mahārāj jī, as well as the regular servants. These ate last.

In the afternoon, people sat around and talked for a few hours. Then Shrivatsa, bathed and dressed in new white clothes, with a tinsel garland around his neck, sat in the inner hall while family members and friends put a mark with red powder on his forehead. When this was over, he and his family went to Rādhāramaṇa temple, and the mourners began to disperse. Everyone who did not live in Jaisingh Ghera was supposed to have left by sundown—though daughters and their families as well as close devotees returned shortly thereafter. In the evening, Shrivatsa and some of the closest friends and family again went with Mahārāj jī to Rādhāramaṇa, carrying a portrait of Mātā jī, to give her darśana of the deity.

The mourning was officially over, but one final ritual was performed. Invitations had been issued to some five hundred Vaiṣṇava men to come for a feast. Feeding brahmans is an obligation frequently mentioned in the *Bhāgavata Purāṇa,* where only men are intended, and it is an act that brings merit, often performed in connection with solemn occasions. The family regularly engages someone who organizes the invitations, asks a certain number from each of various groups, and gives them tickets. Before noon on Saturday (the inauspicious day did not matter, as this was not part of the ritual obligations), the Vaiṣṇavas began to arrive and were seated in rows in the main hall. All could not be accommodated at one time, so some waited for a second seating; about four hundred came all together. After they were seated, someone started passing out the clay cups to each, and then a man went up and down each row, collecting the tickets. He was closely followed by someone else carrying the leaf plates, which were laid in front of the seated men. One man did not have a ticket, and did not get a plate until the organizer was consulted and confirmed that he had, in fact, been invited. The feast consisted largely of fried foods, which can be prepared in large quantities ahead of time, are considered not easily polluted, and are the "party food" associated with feasts and festivals.

After the second seating of Vaiṣṇavas, the family and friends were fed in the inner hall. A few straggling Vaiṣṇavas came in, surrendered their tickets, and were fed. A beggar woman, who had heard there was a feast, came in with them. She had no ticket, but she was recognized and allowed to stay and eat anyway. Again, family and closest devotees fed the others before they also sat down to eat. It is understood as an expression of service and humility to serve the guests; it is also a privilege.

The rituals of the mourning period serve as a period of transition both for the departed soul and for the family and friends left behind. The departed soul is nourished in many ways: with food, by proxy in the person of the priest's wife; by the prayers of the assembled family and friends chanting the sādhānikā hymns; and by material goods, again by proxy. She is inducted into the company of other ancestors, to be remembered and nourished in annual rituals for three generations. This much of the ritual is common practice, as are the conversations consciously and purposely recollecting her life, which console the survivors. The counseling of a guru helps those who have been left behind to remember the true meaning of their lives; this must surely be a practice common to all religions and cultures. The musical offerings were something special to this family. Their dual purpose, like that of all the rituals, was to nourish the departed and the survivors alike.

Thus ended the two weeks of mourning. Death was a reminder of the urgency of Mahārāj jī's teaching.

FOUR

ŚRĪ CAITANYA MAHĀPRABHU

At the core of Mahārāj jī's belief and practice is the figure of Śrī Caitanya Mahāprabhu. The founder of the Caitanyaite Vaiṣṇava sect, he is at once saint, teacher, and deity, for in the understanding of his devotees, Caitanya united in himself three aspects: ecstatic devotee of Krishna, inspired teacher of the love of Krishna, and Krishna himself in inseparable union with Rādhā. He was, in other words, a human being who, by realizing his identity with divinity, became a saint. However, he was also the supreme divinity, who acted upon his desire to experience the bliss that only humans can experience in their love of God. Finally, he was also a teacher, a guru, a bridge between human and divine.[1]

Krishna manifested himself in Vraja in the last world era as a cowherd boy who grew into a charming adolescent; throughout his early life, he inspired a very special love from those around him.[2] Those who loved him most fully were the cowherd women, especially Rādhā; although he enjoyed their love, he wished to experience it himself, so the Caitanyaite Vaiṣṇavas believe that he became manifest in this era as both himself and Rādhā. His name in this incarnation was Caitanya.

The documented historical life of the saint Caitanya reaffirms for his devotees the historical life of Krishna the cowherd boy in Vraja, but in neither case is historicity a privileged category of knowing the truth about them. The truth lies in the relationship with the divine that devotees experience—ānanda, bliss, which completes being (*sat*) and consciousness (*cit*) as constituting the basic nature of both man and God.

Caitanya the Saint

Caitanya was a brilliant child and young man who, at the age of twenty-two, underwent a spiritually transforming experience that led him to devote himself entirely to his relationship with Krishna. He renounced the world but nevertheless organized and directed a renewal of Vaiṣṇava faith during the years of Muslim ascendancy in north India.[3]

His parents lived in a great center of learning, Navadvīpa, on the banks of the Ganges in Bengal, where he was born in 1486 on the night of a full moon—the full moon that marks the spring celebration of Holī—and during a lunar eclipse. He was named Viśvambhara Miśra, though his mother called him Nimāī, and so do his devotees when speaking of him as a child or young man. Six older sisters had died before he was born, and while he was still a child, his elder brother Viśvarūpa left home as a very young man, to become a renunciant, a *sannyāsī*.

Nimāī was a good student and finished his schooling at an early age. After his father, Jagannātha Miśra, died, he became a respected teacher of Sanskrit, teaching in his own school. He married and became a householder. While he was away on a speaking tour—the traditional means by which a teacher collected donations from his followers—his young wife died; he only reluctantly remarried, at his mother's insistence, a young woman named Viṣṇuprīyā.

While Nimāī's father was alive, he would occasionally have long conversations with a pious and learned man, Īśvara Purī, who lived in Gayā, and Nimāī would join in. When Nimāī was twenty-two, he went to Gayā to perform a ritual (*śrāddha*) for his deceased father. There he sought out Īśvara Purī, and the two "had long religious discourses on Krishna, which made [a] lasting impression upon Viśvambhara's mind. He thought he had found out the truth." The elder man initiated the younger, giving him a mantra. "He was completely a changed man, when he returned to Navadvīpa."[4] There are many stories of the young man's growing desire to meet Lord Krishna; merely hearing the name Hari (Krishna) would send him into a state of ecstasy, and his entire appearance would change. Upon recovering himself, he would remember nothing.

From then on, Nimāī associated only with the Vaiṣṇavas of Navadvīpa. They began to worship Krishna in night-long sessions of chanting praise of Krishna, dancing with their arms raised over their heads, accompanied by hand-cymbals and drums slung over the shoulder. The emotion they expressed was love of Krishna, and more particularly the love of Rādhā for Krishna. These private kīrtana sessions, held in the courtyard of the house of one of Nimāī's companions, would end only at dawn. After a while the kīrtana singers began to take their chanting to the streets, by day and night—on the one hand attracting the respect and love of many people by their devotion and on the other provoking the enmity of those who thought them simply to be disturbing the peace. The public kīrtanas, apparently first practical by Nimāī and his friends, were to become the hallmark of the Caitanya Vaiṣṇavas' devotionalism.

At about this time, a young renunciant named Nityānanda arrived in Navadvīpa, saying that he had been directed to seek out Nimāī, whom he had been told was none other than Lord Krishna himself. Nimāī welcomed Nityānanda as if he were his lost elder brother, and the two became the closest of companions. The iconography of Caitanya almost always depicts the two of them together.

After two years of this life, Nimāī determined to become a renunciant (*sannyāsī*) himself, and on January 23, 1510, he took the necessary initiation (*dīkṣā*) from Keśava Bhāratī at Katwa, twenty-four miles from Navadvīpa. Initiation into *sannyāsa* involves renouncing everything of this world—family, possessions, worldly aspirations. There has been some nimble argumentation to explain his taking this vow, since he forbade his followers from doing so. The main explanation is that he did so because within a conservative society his religious vocation would not have been taken seriously if he did not. In any case, those of his followers who have wished to dedicate themselves wholly to participation in Krishna's līlās do not take the full vows of sannyāsa, but a more limited form of renunciation.

At his initiation, Nimāī was given the name Śrī Krishna Caitanya, "he who awakens consciousness of Krishna." A few days after initiation, he went to Puri in Orissa, the site of the great temple of Jagannātha. At the time, Orissa was ruled by a Hindu king, whereas Bengal was ruled by Muslims. Caitanya is reported to have been overcome and fainted when he first had darśana of the deity at Jagannātha temple.

From Puri, Caitanya launched a two-year pilgrimage through south India, where Krishna bhakti (devotionalism) had been developing for several centuries.[5] During this journey, Caitanya seems to have begun planning a new movement of Krishna devotionalism in the north, for he met and recruited some key followers. When he returned to Puri, he stayed there for two more years and then started on a pilgrimage to Vrindaban with a large group of his followers. But because of turbulent political conditions, he was persuaded not to proceed westward with a large group. He returned to Puri, and, after the monsoon, set out again in the autumn of 1515. Traveling with only one companion, he made his way by back roads and forest tracks to Varanasi (where he recruited more followers), then Mathura (Krishna's birthplace), and finally Vrindaban, which he reached on the night of the full moon in November. The night of the November full moon is the night of the great circle dance in the ritual calendar—the culmination of Krishna's youthful relationship with the cowherd women of Vrindaban. Celebrating this occasion on the ritual calendar as well as Caitanya's arrival, on this night a group of Bengali kīrtana singers walk around and through Vrindaban for eight hours, drawing with them an enthusiastic crowd.

In Vrindaban, at this time a nearly deserted area with only a few small settlements, Caitanya stayed for eight months and identified many of the locations where Krishna and Rādhā had sported.[6] This activity was continued and enlarged by others soon thereafter.

Once he was back in Puri, Caitanya stayed for the rest of his life, from 1516 to 1533. He continued to build on the contacts he had made in his travels, however, and to organize his new movement of Krishna devotionalism. Over time, six of his most capable followers whom he sent to establish a center for the worship of Krishna at Vrindaban in the heart of the newly established Mughal empire came to be called the Six Gosvāmīs. Vrindaban became the intellectual and theological center of the movement, although the practice of the kīrtanas and devotionalism itself remained strong traditions in Bengal and Orissa.[7]

For eighteen years, Caitanya spent many hours each day by the Garuḍa pillar in the dancing hall (*nāṭa maṇḍapa*) of the great temple, gazing at Lord Jagannātha. It is said that the imprint of his feet may still be seen in the stone floor, so intense was his presence. He never approached any closer to the deity, perhaps for fear of being totally overwhelmed. The custom of reading Jayadeva's *Gītāgovinda* as part of the daily service in the temple was well established (and continues to this day). This probably inspired Caitanya in his devotion to Rādhā and Krishna. Evidently during his last ten years, the fits of ecstasy he had long been experiencing became more frequent and virtually took over his life: "Often he talked incoherently. Sometimes he shouted, laughed and wept senselessly. Due to emotional frenzy he bruised his face by rubbing it violently on the floor."[8] Exactly how he died is not known, but the most widely accepted story is that one day he left his usual spot by the Garuḍa pillar and actually approached Jagannātha. In the mutual encounter, he merged with the deity.

The facts of Caitanya's life have been elaborated in song, story, and drama. Perhaps the most striking feature of the hagiography are the parallels, both explicit and implicit, between his life and that of the young Krishna in Vrindaban.[9] Caitanya's mother bore six daughters who died before a son was born; the first six children born to Krishna's parents were killed by the wicked king Kaṁsa. Nimāī's elder brother (who was his friend and protector, just like Krishna's elder brother Balarāma) and later his associate Nityānanda are dressed in blue, like Balarāma. The young Caitanya is depicted as a mischievous child who at first refused to study but who eventually proved to be a brilliant student; Krishna, too, did not study until he left Vrindaban but then learned all there was to know in the world in sixty-four days and nights.[10] It is said that the child Nimāī did not accept the conventional worship of the deities but stole and ate the food prepared by his mother for offering. Similarly, Krishna prevented the offering of food to Indra and intercepted food prepared for oblation by the sacrificers' wives.[11] Caitanya was a beautiful boy and young man, who attracted the love and admiration of all who came in contact with him. Unlike Krishna, however, he was not dark complexioned, but golden colored—hence his epithet Gaura or Gaurāṇga (light-hued). The stories that have been made of Caitanya's two years in Navadvīpa after returning from Gayā, leading kīrtana sessions, and of his decision to become a sannyāsī and abandon his young wife and old mother, have an emotional poignancy that parallels the relationship of Krishna with his friends, family, and even Rādhā and the gopīs in Vrindaban.

In Jaisingh Ghera, the presence of Caitanya is not obvious to the casual observer. One would have to hear the private prayers and the kīrtana songs of the women to suspect his presence, and one might notice his picture, along with that of revered, long-dead gurus and various other venerated persons, hung on a wall or propped up on a table. But during six weeks of the monsoon season and for four days at Holī, when the cycles of rāsalīlās are staged at Jaisingh Ghera, Caitanya becomes a central figure. There are two of these dramatic productions each day: in the morning, stories from the life of Caitanya are played; in the evening, from the life of Krishna. Here the dialectic between the two cycles of stories can be appreciated. Caitanya the saint, the ecstatic devotee of Krishna, is presented as a reflection of the young Krishna, who once roamed the forests of Vrindaban. Caitanya's conversion of two notorious town bullies, his winning over the Muslim judge (*qāẓī*) of the town, his meeting with Nityānanda, and his taking the vows of sannyāsa—these and the many other stories of his youth are enacted. Similar themes are also played out by the occasional visiting Bengali storytellers, like the one who performed in the great hall of Jaisingh Ghera during the mourning period for Mātā jī. In a troupe of Vaiṣṇava professionals and businessmen in Bengal who present plays based on the stories of both Caitanya and Krishna (see chapter 6), the actor who plays Krishna also plays Caitanya, the one who plays Balarāma also plays Nityānanda, and the one who plays Rādhā also plays Caitanya's wife, Viṣṇuprīyā.

In most pictures of Caitanya, he is depicted in company with Nityānanda, their long arms raised as they dance, singing the praises of Lord Krishna. But there is another visual depiction of Caitanya, found in a few paintings, and even as the image in a few temples: the six-armed Caitanya (Figure 9). His upper two arms are green and hold the

Figure 9. Painting of Caitanya with six arms.

bow and arrow associated with Rāma, the protagonist of the *Rāmayana* and another avatar of Viṣṇu. The second two arms are blue and hold a flute to his mouth, as Krishna does. The lowest arms are golden, like the rest of Caitanya's body, and hold a mendicant's staff in the right hand and a begging pot in the left. This brings us to the subject of Caitanya as divinity.

Caitanya the Divinity

Caitanya is said to have revealed himself to Nityānanda in his divine, six-armed form when the two first met.[12] But although this six-armed aspect of Caitanya is worshiped in a few temples—one of them maintained by a Rādhāramaṇa Gosvāmī across the street from Rādhāramaṇa Gherā—it is not nearly as widespread as the image of Caitanya with his two arms raised in ecstatic dance. The commingling of Rādhā and Krishna in inseparable embrace, though very occasionally depicted as a body half male, half female, is understood to be represented in the iconography of Caitanya with his golden coloring, like Rādhā, dressed in the yellow clothes that Krishna wears. This perception of Caitanya as both Rādhā and Krishna in one body is what distinguishes Caitanyaite Vaiṣṇavism from other sects of Vaiṣṇavas.

Krishna manifested in Vrindaban, it is said, for two reasons: he wished to relieve the sufferings of the earth (this is the framing story of his appearance in the *Bhāgavata Purāṇa*), and he wished to experience for himself the sweetness of Rādhā's love for him (this is the teaching of the Caitanyaite Vaiṣṇavas). This latter rationale, on the surface a sentimental conceit, is in fact the tip of a theological and metaphysical iceberg. For Rādhā (together with the cowherd women, who are an extension of her) is Krishna's *śakti,* his divine energy; the two cannot exist apart from one another, and the play of the two is what creates the world.[13] The relationship of the two is *prema* (love), and through prema they experience ānanda (bliss).

It was in Vrindaban that Krishna and Rādhā could enjoy one another's love, and the love of Rādhā and her friends for Krishna became the model to which Vaiṣṇava devotees could aspire in their spiritual practice. But Krishna, it is said, wanted to know himself what it was like to be Rādhā and experience such love, for she alone was able to love God fully. This is why he resolved to incarnate in the Kali yuga, the present world era, as both himself and Rādhā in a single body. That incarnation was Caitanya, who was Rādhā on the outside (thus his extraordinary golden color), and Krishna within. Krishna of Vrindaban was, in popular imagery of poem and song, the golden moon; Caitanya, born during a lunar eclipse, was called in Bengali poetry the dark moon. (Shrivatsa Goswami explains that when the moon is dark, it is most fully known in itself, with no dependence on the light of the sun, and is thus most complete.)

Indian religious traditions acknowledge, explore, and cultivate the experience of ānanda—the creative, nourishing force translated in English as bliss—as a fundamental attribute of reality, on a par with being (*sat*) and consciousness (*cit*): sat-cit-ānanda. To seek to understand the inner logic of ānanda through discipline (*sādhana*) is accepted as a valid and important spiritual path, and by Vaiṣṇavas as the only fruitful path in our age. The aim of this path is to bring about a change in oneself through self-control, which will permit one to experience ānanda in the midst of life, without abandoning one's responsibilities in the world.[14]

Vaiṣṇava tradition accepts sat-cit-ānanda as defining characteristics of both God and man, and thus immediately the two are related by a network of correspondences. There are various accepted spiritual paths to explore and understand this network. One widely followed path is the path of knowledge (*jñāna*). As Shrivatsa Goswami explicates this path, those who follow it assume that the object of one's search—truth as Being (*sat*)—is real and transcendent, and that oneself as seeker is not real, or only contingently real. If the goal of pure knowledge were to be achieved, the seeker would be liberated—erased—and only the ultimate, transcendent reality of being would remain. There is no question of a relationship between the two.[15]

The other traditional path is that of deeds (*karma*), the way of the yogi. In the same argument, those who follow this discipline take the seeker to be real; the aim is to liberate his pure consciousness (*cit*) from attachment to the external world of contingent reality. If this goal were to be reached, the external would be erased, and only the ultimate, transcendent reality of consciousness would remain.

The way of devotion (*bhakti*), by this argument, takes as its reality the relationship between subject and object, and its goal is not liberation but full realization of this relationship (*ānanda*). The relationship can be conceived of as the līlā of Krishna, his divine play; the stories of Krishna's life in Vrindaban are vehicles for realizing the relationship of love between human and divine, which is the ultimate reality of human existence. Rādhā and the cowherd women were the perfect knowers of that love; Uddhava, when he met with them on the riverbank, recognized the power of their experience of love but did not know how to establish a real relationship with the divine. Krishna, in the form of the black bee, appeared to help him bow down to the feet of the women. At this moment, Krishna, the black bee, acted as the guru. It is the guru who acts as the transformer of the energy of the relationship between human and divine, making each accessible to the other.

Caitanya as Guru

At the beginning of any formal discourse by Shrivatsa, divine intercession is invoked by the singing of a chant whose chorus runs: "Jaya [hail] Nityānanda, jaya Gauracandra [golden moon, epithet of Caitanya], jaya Rādhāramaṇa [and in subsequent verses Rādhā-Govinda, Rādhā-Gopinātha, and Rādhā linked with other names of Krishna], Jaya jaya hai!" Caitanya here is invoked as the guru, the one who makes possible the entrance of ānanda into the gathering of devotees. The predominant mood of a *Bhāgavata* discourse, and what the listeners are supposed to gain from it, is ānanda. Ānanda exists in the present moment, uniting being and consciousness. It is the way of the companions of Rādhā (*sakhīs*), who serve her only to enable the divine couple to enjoy ānanda. The guru is understood to play this same role by virtue of his own practice and by the fact that he has been initiated into direct service of the divine couple in the temple. In following this path, he has moved more closely than most to the divine, and as such he is also considered a saint.

Following the "fuzzy logic" of metaphor, Shrivatsa explains that the incarnation of Krishna (*avatāra*) represents a movement of the divine toward humanity and that the spiritual path of a saint is a movement of the human toward the divine. The guru is, in this metaphor, the initiated, experienced teacher who serves as a bridge between the two. Just as the priest in the temple mediates between deity and worshiper through service and ritual, so the guru mediates between the eternal (*nitya*) and the revealed (*prakaṭa*) and prepares the devotee to experience both. This role, that of the teacher, is the primary role of Caitanya in the Caitanyaite Vaiṣṇava tradition. What Caitanya teaches is Rādhā's experience of the love for Krishna; the experience of ānanda (bliss) in their union is the salvation that his followers seek.

Caitanya's elevation of Rādhā to a preeminent position in the worship of Krishna was a crucial turning point in the revival of Vaiṣṇavism. But perhaps even more crucial was the example he set of the path of bhakti, loving devotion to the divinity and participation in his līlās, and the strong organization of that form of worship, which ensured the survival of his vision for five hundred years.

There is yet another image that is closely associated with Śrī Caitanya Mahāprabhu: the image of Rādhāramaṇa, "he who enjoys Rādhā," said to be another form of the incarnation of Rādhā and Krishna in one body, and whose appearance was invoke'd by Gopāla Bhaṭṭa. Whereas in Caitanya, Rādhā was on the outside and Krishna inside, in the black stone image of Rādhāramaṇa, Krishna is outside, Rādhā inside. Thus the Rādhāramaṇa Gosvāmīs hold the temple of Śrī Rādhāramaṇa to be the highest seat of Caitanyaite Vaiṣṇava worship, and it lies at the center of their devotional life.

FIVE

RĀDHĀRAMAṆA TEMPLE

Service to the Deity

Śrī Rādhāramaṇa, a small black figure only eleven and one-eighth inches high, stands in a relaxed pose with his hands raised to hold a flute to his lips—although, in fact, those hands are never seen to hold a flute. Rādhāramaṇa's right hand always holds a cowherd's staff, by which he is seen to support himself (Figure 10). He is the oldest image of Krishna in Vrindaban that has never had to leave. Housed in a small temple a block or two from Jaisingh Ghera, he is served by the lineage of Gosvāmīs that includes Mahārāj jī's family. The story of the origin of this image has its roots in the visit of Caitanya to the holy city of Śrīraṅgam near Tiruchirapalli during his tour of south India.[1]

History of Rādhāramaṇa

Śrī Caitanya arrived at Śrīraṅgam at the beginning of the monsoon season, when religious wanderers traditionally remain in one place during four months. Caitanya decided to stay in the home of one of the main temple priests of Śrīraṅgam, Śrī Vaiṅkaṭa Bhaṭṭa. During those four months, according to tradition, the saint was impressed with the qualities of Śrī Vaiṅkaṭa Bhaṭṭa's young son Gopāla, and the child, in turn, made up his mind to take Caitanya as his spiritual guide.

When Gopāla Bhaṭṭa came of age, Śrī Caitanya set him the task of traveling to the border of Nepal, to the source of the Kali Gaṇḍakī River, to bring back several *śālagrāma* stones—special river-washed,

Figure 10. Rādhāramaṇa dressed for hot weather. Photo by Jagadish Lāl Gosvāmī; courtesy of Pravin Photo House, Vrindaban.

rounded black stones containing ammonites, revered by Vaiṣṇavas as manifestations of the deity. After a difficult trek, Gopāla Bhaṭṭa reached the lake called Dāmodarakuṇḍa, on what is now the Tibetan border of Nepal in Mustang district, where the most valued śālagrāmas are found. From there, carrying his precious śālagrāmas, he returned via Saharanpur district in Uttar Pradesh and passed through the town now called Deoband. There he acquired three worthy disciples, including the Gauḍa brahman Gopīnātha and his younger brother, Dāmodara.

Śrī Caitanya had already sent several followers to Vrindaban to establish Krishna's worship there, and Gopāla Bhaṭṭa joined them. For years, he assiduously worshiped his śālagrāmas, and at Śrī Caitanya's request composed an encyclopedic compendium describing the way of life to be followed by a Caitanyaite Vaiṣṇava, the *Haribhaktivilāsa*, as well as other works. Caitanya, in general, gave initiation (*dikṣā*) to no one; that is, he took no ritually established disciples—he taught that a renunciant should acquire nothing, even disciples. He seems to have made one exception, however, and made Gopāla Bhaṭṭa his initiated disciple. As a result, Gopāla Bhaṭṭa was the only one of the Six Gosvāmīs who established a lineage of disciples. As an indication of Gopāla Bhaṭṭa's position, Śrī Caitanya Mahāprabhu sent his own seat (*āsana*), his necklace (*mālā*), and renunciate's loin cloth (*kaupīna*) to this holy man of Vrindaban.

After many years of worship, in 1542, it is said that Gopāla Bhaṭṭa had become discouraged because Śrī Caitanya's promise made years before (he had left the world in 1533) had not yet been fulfilled. This was the promise that Gopāla Bhaṭṭa would have his, Caitanya's, darśana (equivalent, in Gopāla Bhaṭṭa's belief, to darśana of Śrī Krishna and Rādhā themselves) through worship of the śālagrāma stones. On the eve of Buddha Jayanti, the full moon of Vaiśākha (April–May), Gopāla Bhaṭṭa was reading the sacred story of the young boy Prahlāda, to whom Krishna manifested in the form of the man-lion Nṛsiṃha. Gopāla Bhaṭṭa was overwhelmed by the realization that this young boy had the good fortune to see the Lord himself through the power of his devotion, but that he himself had not been so fortunate. Acutely feeling his own worthlessness, he lost consciousness. A basket holding the precious śālagrāmas was hanging from a branch overhead. When he regained consciousness, he noticed that the lid of the basket had come open a bit. Fearing that a snake had entered, he tried to push down the lid but found it impossible to do so. Then he looked inside and found, instead of the śālagrāmas, a small black figure, his head tipped slightly to the left, his torso leaning slightly to the right from a slender waist, his knees gracefully bent and his right foot crossed over his left. This "triple-bent" (*tribhaṅga*) boy was holding a flute to his lips with both hands. This is the image whose home is in Rādhāramaṇa temple. It is understood that he is the same as the deity Gopāla Bhaṭṭa had longed to see—Śrī Caitanya Mahāprabhu, the incarnation of Rādhā and Krishna in one body. The proof that this is a self-revealed image that originated from a śālagrāma is said to be that it bears on its back the gold-flecked imprint of the original Dāmodara śālagrāmas—although no one but an initiated priest of the temple is allowed to see Rādhāramaṇa's back. It is also argued that it could not have been carved because if a cutting tool is applied to a śālagrāma it will simply flake away.

This was an era when other manifestations of Krishna were being discovered in Vrindaban and elsewhere in Vraja. In about 1534, Rūpa Gosvāmī discovered the image of Govindadeva, about four feet tall, on the hill where the great temple of Govindadeva now stands.[2] Probably within the same decade his brother Sanātana identified the image of Madanamohana and installed it in a temple on another hill.[3] And there were many others. All these images of Krishna were the personal deities of the saints who were founders of Caitanyaite Vaiṣṇavism in Vrindaban. Like the thousands of other images that over time became enshrined as the personal deities of devotees, they were entrusted to the care of the immediate families and heirs of those who established them. Temples and shrines of every size, from spacious courtyards down to small household niches or altars, were built and maintained by these families, and Vrindaban is known for these thousands of shrines. A handful of these deities—Madanamohana, Govindadeva, and Rādhāramaṇa among them—also became foci for the devotion of a wider community. The temples continue to the present day to belong to the heirs of the founders (though they are protected by civil law and cannot be sold as private property), but they attract a circle of regular devotees from the town, as well as pilgrims who come from afar.

Sevā in the temple, service to Rādhāramaṇa, is maintained by members of the group of Gosvāmī families who trace their lineage to Gopāla Bhaṭṭa. The first link in the chain of inheritance is spiritual, not physical. Gopāla Bhaṭṭa never married, and although he asked his elder disciple, Gopīnātha, to start a family, the latter also remained unmarried and followed a life of spiritual practice in his guru's footsteps. The demand to found a line of priests to serve Rādhāramaṇa jī then fell upon Gopīnātha's brother Dāmodara. Dāmodara married and had three sons, the eldest of whom also had three sons; these three grandsons of Dāmodara and their two uncles founded the five lineages of Gosvāmīs who currently serve at the temple. (A cousin of Gopīnātha and Dāmodara,

Śrī Hit Harivaṃśa, who also settled in Vrindaban and who founded the Rādhāvallabha sect, also initially took to a renunciate's life but subsequently married. This provided a marriage pool for the lineages of Gosvāmīs in both the Rādhāramaṇa and Rādhāvallabha temples at Vrindaban, and elsewhere as well.)[4] In principle, service (*sevā*) in Rādhāramaṇa is equally divided among the five lineages, and within them among the forty-odd families of Rādhāramaṇa Gosvāmīs, and is shared by all initiated males in the lineages. The crucial moment of this initiation involves touching the feet of the deity after proper preparation, and only those who have done so are privileged to have intimate contact with him. Inheritance of the right to receive initiation passes through the male line only; the sons of a daughter cannot serve in the temple.

Most of the priests who serve in Rādhāramaṇa temple have traditionally lived within Rādhāramaṇa Gherā (compound). The protecting walls, however, have never prevented the Gosvāmīs from traveling extensively. Many families have a tradition of learning and culture, and sons have left to study before returning to practice and teach. Many have also moved away, returning only when it is their time to serve in the temple (or they may arrange for one of the Gosvāmīs living in Rādhāramaṇa Gherā to do the rituals on their behalf). Some have gone on to earn a living in secular jobs; others serve Rādhāramaṇa temples in the diaspora. The Gosvāmīs of Rādhāramaṇa have always had close ties to a number of cities and towns throughout north India, and in many of these there are Rādhāramaṇa temples that were built by followers of one or another guru within the Vrindaban lineage. There are thus Rādhāramaṇa Gosvāmīs in Patna, Varanasi, Pilibhit, Bareilly, Farrukhabad, Bharatpur, Shahjahanpur, Kanpur, Allahabad, Surat, and elsewhere who still maintain their position at Rādhāramaṇa in Vrindaban. Some sublineages have communities of disciples scattered across north and west India.

The story of how the Rādhāramaṇa temple at Pilibhit was founded exemplifies the growth of the diaspora. One of Mahārāj jī's devotees is from Pilibhit, a town about a hundred miles east of Delhi, not far from Bareilly. Her great-grandfather, the owner of a sugar factory, had no sons. He and his wife went to hear a discourse by a Rādhāramaṇa Gosvāmī, and soon afterward she delivered a boy. The happy factory owner founded a temple, and a Gosvāmī from Rādhāramaṇa temple in Vrindaban came to be the priest. But the story does not end there. It seems that over the years the Gosvāmīs in Pilibhit abandoned some of their Vaiṣṇava ways and joined in the luxurious and dissolute ways of the founder's family. But in the next generation one of the sons was a simple man, a vegetarian and abstainer who married a woman from a Varanasi family whose members were devotees of Mahārāj jī. One daughter of this marriage is the devotee of Mahārāj jī. There seems, she says, to be one person in each generation of this family who carries on the sevā in the temple; others might attend special events, such as discourses held there, but do not otherwise follow a Vaiṣṇava way of life or are only partially observant.

As for the two sons and three grandsons of Dāmodara, each took responsibility for sevā at the temple for six months at a time, so each had a turn every two and a half years. This rotation has been passed down through the generations, and within each sublineage the six months have been successively subdivided.[5] One sublineage has only one surviving representative, so his turn lasts six months. The other families within the line of succession have much shorter terms. Mahārāj jī's father, for example, had sixty-six days. Mahārāj jī was only eleven years old when, after his father's death, his family's turn for sevā came around. He was obviously not able to conduct the sevā himself, but he organized others to act on behalf of the family. Later, the sixty-six days were divided equally among the three brothers. Mahārāj jī performs sevā for his twenty-two days jointly with his two sons (and, as of 1997, two grandsons). About five months before these twenty-two days, Mahārāj jī has another week of sevā; one family within the sublineage to which he belongs died out, and their time was divided among other families in the sublineage.

These periods of sevā are times of great spiritual concentration and fulfillment for the Gosvāmīs. They wish to offer the best of anything within their resources that can be prepared for Krishna's enjoyment. All else in their lives flows from this.

The Temple of Rādhāramaṇa

Unlike many deities, Rādhāramaṇa has never left the temple that is his home. And it is built to look like a home. Many of the shrines of Vrindaban, in fact, are integral parts of the family houses; they are platforms built along one side of a courtyard whose other three sides hold the family's living quarters, or the living quarters are built above and behind the deity's shrine. Seen from the outside, Rādhāramaṇa might seem to be just another of these household shrines. It is nestled at the back of a compound, Rādhāramaṇa Gherā, which one enters from the street through a massive doorway with heavy wooden doors that are closed at night. The compound courtyard is lined with the houses of Gosvāmīs. To the left, just inside the gate, is a small passageway that gives access to a red sandstone archway and a shrine marking the spot where Rādhāramaṇa revealed himself. A tree next to the archway is identified as the very tree in which the basket of śālagrāmas hung. Next door, there is a memorial shrine of Gopāla Bhaṭṭa and all the deceased Gosvāmīs.

If one walks straight across the courtyard from the gate, without turning into the passageway with the memorial shrine, one can then turn left, go through another massive doorway with heavy wooden doors, and enter another courtyard lined with more houses. A few steps inside the courtyard, there is a communal pump on one side, often with children playing around it, people washing their hands or feet, or someone drawing water in a bucket. Now one is facing Rādhāramaṇa temple itself, a simple sandstone structure at first glance hardly distinguishable from the houses around it (Figure 11). Behind it, still out of sight to

Figure 11. Rādhāramaṇa temple. Photo by Robyn Beeche.

the visitor and accessible by a narrow passageway behind the temple, is the small building originally built for Rādhāramaṇa in the late sixteenth century.[6] This was supplemented after some time by a somewhat larger one built next to it. Both are very plain, small buildings, now used as the kitchen, dining room, and bedroom for the deity.

Because of this discretion in building design and the small size of the image, which could easily be hidden, Rādhāramaṇa never had to be removed during the political disorders of the seventeenth century, when larger images of the deity left Vrindaban for the safety of Rajput territory; Govindadeva, Gopīnātha, Vinodīlāla, and Rādhā Dāmodara, for example, are still in Jaipur.

In the nineteenth century, there was an influx of wealth and a spate of building in Vrindaban, and Rādhāramaṇa was one of the beneficiaries. Then, as now, devotees of Rādhāramaṇa were spread over a wide area. One of the more prominent ones was Shah Kundan Lal, finance minister of Wajid Ali Shah, the last Nawab of Avadh. When the Nawab was defeated by the British and Shah Kundan Lal lost his position, he turned his attention and resources to his deity in Vrindaban. First, he built what he felt to be the most beautiful temple that money could buy. The result was a hybrid edifice of Italian marble "fronted with a colonnade of spiral marble pillars, each shaft being of a single piece, which though rather too attenuated are unquestionably elegant," wrote a late nineteenth-century British observer. "The mechanical execution is also good; but all is rendered to no avail by the abominable taste of the design. The facade with its uncouth pediment, flanked by sprawling monsters, and its row of life-size female figures in meretricious, but at the same time most ungraceful attitudes, resembles nothing so much as a disreputable London casino. . . . Ten lakhs of rupees are said to have been wasted on its construction."[7]

The Gosvāmīs of Rādhāramaṇa temple declined to allow their deity to move to this lavish new temple, and Shah Kundan Lal resigned himself to building the modest sandstone temple that is now Rādhāramaṇa's home.[8] The gaudy marble Shahji Mandir, which stands on the other side of Jaisingh Ghera from Rādhāramaṇa Gherā, and whose massive courtyard walls tower over the street that leads from Jaisingh Ghera to the bazaar, is maintained chiefly as an attraction for pilgrims and tourists. As such, the ambience of a busy pilgrim site prevails: stalls with mementos crowd around the courtyard entrance, including four or five that sell cassettes with songs celebrating Rādhā and Krishna, set to popular and *filmi* tunes, competing with each other in a decibel war that deafens the passerby.

A notable feature of the small plaza and steps in front of Shahji Mandir is the abundance of brazen monkeys, who are fed by the pilgrims. They swarm over this area, as well as Jaisingh Ghera and Nidhiban, a wild garden area enclosed by high walls, a few yards away—the place where the popular deity Baṅke Bihārī was discovered by the saint Haridāsa in about 1534, and one of the places where Rādhā and Krishna are said to have their nightly trysts. The monkeys steal anything one might be carrying, especially food, and are skilled at snatching glasses off the faces of passersby. If the monkey stays within range, it can usually be tempted to return the glasses in exchange for food, and the merchants at the stalls around the temple do a brisk business retrieving pilgrims' "specs" for a fee of ten rupees.

The crowds, the merchants, and the blaring music are all absent from the ambience of the present temple of Rādhāramaṇa The first harbinger of change appeared in 1994, when a video rental store opened in the small plaza just outside Rādhāramaṇa Gherā—but it does not broadcast its programs. (In 1997, a small shop selling items to decorate one's personal deities at home opened inside the compound, at the foot of the steps to the temple itself, but it was closed within a few months.) Rādhāramaṇa temple, built of the same light pink sandstone as most of Vrindaban's nineteenth-century buildings, nestles comfortably among the houses around the quiet compound. The simple doorway on the south side of the temple, under a sign in Hindi and English identifying it, is flanked by two standing male figures holding lotus buds. Just inside is a small vestibule, where shoes and socks are to be left—for none may be worn in the temple—and to the right a small flight of four steps leads to the interior of the temple.

The temple is built around an inner courtyard about thirty-five feet square, partially open to the sky but at night and in bad weather covered by a sliding tin roof. This style of temple architecture, known as the *havelī* style, derives from a common form of domestic architecture in the region—one, two, or three stories built around an inner courtyard. The floor of Rādhāramaṇa temple is a checkerboard of black and white marble. On the left as you enter, there is a marble platform about four and a half feet high, and behind it is the inner sanctum. The courtyard is surrounded on the other three sides by porticos, each with three arches that were recently painted a slightly surprising bright pink and green. Even when the doors to the inner sanctum are closed, and the deity is not visible, a few devotees are usually to be found sitting in the porticos or standing around in the courtyard, perhaps chatting with one another. In the rear (east) portico, facing the sanctum, a singer sits in the morning and evening with a harmonium, perhaps with a tabla (drum) player or with other devotees who keep time with hand cymbals as he sings chants of praise to Krishna.

The raised platform that serves as the antechamber to the inner sanctum also has three cusped arches, these of unpainted sandstone; at the rear is an embossed silver double-leaved door leading to the sanctum. There the deity stands facing east. For about a century, two sets of stairs led from the courtyard up to the platform, and worshipers could go up for close darśana of the deity. When the Temple Entry Act was passed by the British, requiring that temples be open to all Hindus regardless of caste, the stairs were removed, and now only Gosvāmīs and temple servants go up to the platform. In the hot weather and on certain festival days, the deity is brought out to the platform so as to allow his devotees closer access to him.

The Sevā at Rādhāramaṇa Temple

Sevā of Rādhāramaṇa involves service to the deity throughout the day by priests who are mindful of his eternal, daily activities, which are considered to take place at specific times during the eight periods or watches into which the day is divided. They wake him up, prepare him for darśana, bathe and dress him, feed him, and honor him with rituals that are collectively called pūjā (worship). The rituals honoring the deity are precise and in principle unalterable, constituting a logic of relationship between the person conducting the pūjā and the deity.[9] The pūjā conducted in public is called *āratī*—a term that refers to the circling of lighted wicks in front of the deity, a token of the devotion being offered, but is commonly taken to mean the public portion of the priests' attendance on him with offerings of other items as well.

The temple is opened before dawn; the first āratī, *maṅgala ārati*, is at 4:45 or 5:00 A.M. in the summer, 5:30 A.M. in winter. The temple is locked at night, and the key is in the safekeeping of the Gosvāmī who is in charge of sevā at the time. Sometimes, something goes awry. One summer morning in 1994, for example, the key could not be found. When it was finally located, it would not turn in the keyhole. Not until 6:00 or 7:00 A.M. were the Gosvāmīs able to enter and prepare Rādhāramaṇa for darśana. The whole compound was abuzz, of course, and it was rumored that for the rest of the day Rādhāramaṇa jī had a happy grin on his face.[10]

Normally, the first darśana of the day is announced by the ringing of the temple bell. Soon after the Gosvāmīs have awakened Rādhāramaṇa and prepared him for darśana, there is a short peal in the predawn darkness and five minutes later, a clanging that continues throughout the service. On most mornings, perhaps a dozen neighbors have gathered when the bell first rings; perhaps two dozen more come in after the first ringing, and more enter as the service proceeds. Many are women who have already taken their morning baths and come with their little pots of Yamunā water that they will use for their own devotions at home. Many bring little wicks soaked in oil to light on the edge of the platform before the deity; most toss small coins or flowers onto the platform during the service. Outside the temple sits a man who sells flower garlands for a rupee or two, which some devotees buy and place on a low stool at the front of the platform as an offering to Rādhāramaṇa. Others bring tulasī leaves to place there.

Before the doors to the inner sanctum are opened, many of the people who come to greet him circumambulate the inner sanctum, walking behind the temple (keeping it to their right), entering a back door on the northwest corner of the temple, walking clockwise around the courtyard inside the temple and out the main entrance, and turning right again to go behind the temple. Each has a specific number of times he or she customarily goes around, repeating a mantra all the while. Meanwhile, the men who have gathered inside sit on the checkered marble floor and sing *bhajanas*—chants evoking Krishna and Rādhā—with the harmonium player in the rear portico. The women tend to sit within the shelter of the porticos. When movement on the platform indicates that the curtains in front of the deity are about to be opened, all stand up and move to the front of the court, and there is a certain dramatic tension as people wait for the curtain to be opened so they can see the deity, awakened for the new day.

At Rādhāramaṇa's first darśana he is still wearing his night clothes, including in the winter a little flat-topped cap that covers his ears, like those worn by the men who come to worship him, and a warm shawl; his tiny form is literally adorable. He is simultaneously a small child and the resplendent Lord. He stands on a small embossed golden platform, which is, in turn, placed on an embossed silver throne with lion feet. These were all made by a silversmith family that lives and works in a passageway off the plaza outside Rādhāramaṇa Gherā. Below the throne are placed various silver figures that have been presented to the deity by devotees—cows, swans, pots, and so on. These are arranged, generally symmetrically, at the discretion of the priests. Over Rādhāramaṇa's head a small golden umbrella is balanced.

On Rādhāramaṇa's left side, the nonfigurative representation of Rādhā (a cloth draped over a form, topped by a jeweled crown) is clothed with a sari of the same fabric that Krishna's clothes are made of. Rādhā is also shaded by a small golden umbrella. (Since Rādhāramaṇa is the incarnation of Rādhā and Krishna together, a separate figurative image of her would be redundant; but she is represented, nevertheless—*acintyabhedābeda*.) Only two other temples in Vrindaban observe service of the seat of Rādhā without her figurative presence: Rādhāvallabha and Baṅke Bihārī.[11]

To Rādhāramaṇa's right in the inner sanctum, mostly out of sight to those standing in the temple courtyard, is another golden umbrella that shades a stool holding the remaining śālagrāmas of Gopāla Bhaṭṭa, and behind that is a small throne with the stool that Caitanya Mahāprabhu presented to Gopāla Bhaṭṭa. (The necklace he presented to Gopāla Bhaṭṭa has disintegrated; only a small piece of the loincloth remains, framed in silver, and it appears in public on Rādhāramaṇa's day of appearance and on Janmaṣṭami, Krishna's birthday, as well as on a very few other days.) All four loci of divinity—Rādhāramaṇa, śālagrāmas, Rādhā, and Caitanya's seat—are offered āratī in succession.

In the early morning, this service is short and simple. The bell clangs overhead, and a pair of sonorous gongs is sounded to the side of the arcaded platform; the sound invades the body and seems to come up through the feet of those standing inside the temple. The priest first waves a silver holder with three wooden tapers wrapped in fine cotton batting, soaked in oil, and lighted. Holding it in his right hand, he traces out the letters of the sacred sound "OM." With his left hand, he holds and rings a silver handbell, and he chants a liturgy of mantras to each of the holy loci in the sanctum. This done, the priest puts down the lights, and the clanging of the bell stops; he goes "backstage," fetches a basin of water and a cloth, and cleans the platform where he has been. One of the Gosvāmīs serving Rādhāramaṇa comes to take up the garlands and tulasī leaves that have been left on the low stool at the front of the platform to offer to the deity. The devotees—particularly now the women—begin to sing their own chants of devotion. On the platform, small rituals continue until, after a few minutes, the doors of the sanctum close.

The people disperse to their morning routines. The priests also perform the daily routines with Krishna—they carefully and lovingly bathe, dress, and feed Rādhāramaṇa. Now and throughout the day, priests and devotees keep in mind the activities of the divine couple. The devotees aspire to serve the deities in their hearts continually and without interruption;

Figure12. Reading the *Bhāgavatā Purāṇa*, Rādhāramaṇa temple, December. 1994.

the priests do so physically—which is why sevā is so highly cherished as a privilege and opportunity.

During Mahārāj jī's sevā, the first service the devotees have the opportunity to perform takes place in the predawn darkness, after maṅgala āratī is finished. A few devotees sweep and wash all the floors of the temple. The debris is put in a pile that is thrown into the Yamunā River, for disposing of it by any other means, including burning, would be considered an offense to the deity. Then, as the sky begins to lighten and daylight seeps into the temple, they set up the low tables and seats for the reading of the *Bhāgavata Purāṇa* that begins when it is light. Fourteen or sometimes twenty-eight Caitanyaite brahmans, carefully selected by Mahārāj jī, sit at low tables in the central court, facing the sanctum, each reading one-fourteenth of the *Bhāgavata* aloud—simultaneously but not in unison—so that each day the entire text is read (Figure 12). Meanwhile, eleven or twenty-two readers sitting on the side porticos read the *Nārāyaṇa kavaca* (book VI.8 of the *Bhāgavata Purāṇa),* whereby all the names and attributes of the Lord Nārāyaṇa are recited, and protection is sought from each.

The reading lasts for about two and a half hours, during which a few devotees drift in, having bathed and breakfasted after maṅgala āratī. Many of them proceed with their own devotions: reciting mantras or reading a text that had been suggested to them by Mahārāj jī. When the *Bhāgavata* readers have all finished, they close their copies of the text, and devotees pass among them, honoring the *Bhāgavata Purāṇa* and the readers with garlands, marks of sandalwood paste on their foreheads (*tilaka*), little leaf dishes of fruits and sweets, and an envelope with a few rupees. The listening devotees also receive the tilaka.

Then the readers' low tables are cleared and stored in a side room, and cotton rugs are spread on the marble floor for devotees to sit on and listen to the music that follows, played by musicians siting in the rear (east) portico. Soon Mahārāj jī and Shrivatsa come out onto the platform, in front of the closed curtain, and talk quietly with devotees who come up to them with questions or greetings or to make further arrangements for the sevā. Each day an individual devotee or a small family group offers pūjā to Rādhāramaṇa, standing in front of the platform while Mahārāj jī recites mantras and guides them in the ritual offerings (Figure 13). The devotees who do this pay a handsome amount for the opportunity, which is one source of the funds for this very expensive operation.

Each pūjā conducted by Mahārāj jī follows a set pattern. First an earthenware pot containing water is placed on the platform. An assistant has a brass tray with the other materials. Mahārāj jī mixes some water with red powder to make a paste; with his guidance, the person on

Figure 13. Mahārāj jī doing a pūjā , Rādhāramaṇa temple, December 1994.

whose behalf the pūjā was being done ties a piece of string (*kalāvā*)—hand-spun cotton dyed in bands with red powder and turmeric—around the neck of the pot. Then the assistant or the person doing the pūjā makes a *svastika*, an auspicious mark, on the pot. Fresh leaves from five kinds of trees are placed in the pot, with a fresh coconut on top. Two bits of the string are tied on the leaves, and a leaf is used to dip out four portions of water on the leaves. All this time, Mahārāj jī is reciting mantras. Then a pinch of powder and a few unbroken grains of rice are added. A garland of flowers is placed on the leaves in the pot. Finally, the devotee lights a wick in a small dish of ghi and performs āratī. Next a svastika is drawn with the red paste on the platform, a garland is placed around it, and sometimes rupees are put in the middle. Mahārāj jī's benediction follows, and often he speaks for some time with the person or group doing the pūjā.

Meanwhile, behind the doors of the sanctum, Rādhāramaṇa has his morning bath in Yamunā water, and after he has been served his freshly cooked breakfast—unlike most deities, he is physically moved to the inner rooms for these activities—Rādhāramaṇa is dressed in new finery for the day. There is a regular calendar of colors for the temple: Sunday is red, Monday pink, Tuesday coral, Wednesday green, Thursday yellow, Friday white or multicolored, Saturday dark blue or black. These are the colors associated with the sun, moon, and planets that the days are named after. The priests may choose any costume for Rādhāramaṇa from the wardrobe in the temple's storerooms, often in the color of the day, though this is not obligatory. Or a devotee may donate a costume to be used on a given day (the costume is accompanied by a substantial financial donation). The outfit includes many pieces: a costume for Rādhāramaṇa himself, a *dupaṭṭā* (scarf), a shawl, and a drape for the back of the throne. There is also a sari and a shawl for Rādhā. On Rādhāramaṇa's head is a turban or crown, always with a peacock feather. During Mahārāj jī's sevā, a new costume of fine silk, richly embroidered in silver and gold, adorns Rādhāramaṇa each day, and new headdresses are also created. The variety of pieces allows for innumerable combinations of colors and textures in the fabric and embroidery (Figure 14).

After Rādhāramaṇa is dressed, he is further adorned with jewelry and flowers. In the temple's collection are some fine pieces of antique jewelry—necklaces, earrings, bracelets and anklets, belts and girdles for both the deity and his consort. New jewelry, always designed by Mahārāj jī, is donated on the occasion of Mahārāj jī's sevā and joins the diamonds, precious stones, pearls, and gold in the collection.

The darśana at midmorning (*dhūpa ārati*), after Rādhāramaṇa is dressed

Figure 14. Rādhāramaṇa jī. Photo by Jagadish Lāl Gosvāmī; courtesy of Pravin Photo House, Vrindaban.

for the day, is eagerly anticipated by the devotees. When the weather is cool, both Rādhāramaṇa and the devotees are now in colorful silks as they gaze at each other. Several of the women make a point of dressing in the "color of the day." A few of the devotees have binoculars, which are passed around and greedily snapped up by other viewers in the crowd, who admire his beauty and point out the special details to one another. The mood is one of a large extended family that has gathered to honor a very beloved and respected, but not always accessible, senior member. Many of the viewers are simply absorbed in taking in the vision of divine beauty. The āratī at this time is offered with a cotton wick light, and also with aloe and sandalwood charcoal incense (*dhūpa*), and again the bells are rung.

For each successive darśana (viewing the deity, both during āratī and otherwise), Rādhāramaṇa's basic costume remains the same, but details of adornment change, and in the evening lush garlands of flowers may be added.

A crucial step in the preparation of Rādhāramaṇa each day is the placing of his eyes, which are white elongated petal shapes that stand out against his jet-black face. They, like his other adornments, are fixed to his form with softened beeswax, and they are the last thing to be put on him when he is dressed. The black irises transfix the viewer. And his eyes are not the only things that change; sometimes two small white teeth can be seen in the center of his smile, or a bit of butter shows in the corner of his mouth after his breakfast. Just as they see Rādhāramaṇa smile when he is especially pleased and do not ask how, devotees do not ask how his teeth can sometimes be seen. But if his upper lip is made shiny with oil, it is quite possible that it will reflect the lustrous pearl or gold beads of his necklace.

The āratīs conducted later in the day are more elaborate than the first two in the morning. In mid morning, at *śṛṅgāra āratī*, while the bell clangs and the gongs are sounded, the priest first offers handfuls of tulasī leaves, grown in the gardens of Vrindaban, from a plate he holds in his left hand, to each of the loci of divinity as he recites the appropriate mantras; each handful is then placed in a bowl at Rādhāramaṇa's feet. Then the taper holder, with more tapers than in the earlier āratīs, is waved (Figure 15), and water in a silver conch shell is waved in the same "OM" pattern, three times, to remove the heat. (Each āratī involves different numbers of tapers, up to a maximum of nine in the early evening.) After he has offered the water, the priest comes to the front of the platform and flings out handfuls of it from the conch shell to sprinkle the assembled devotees as a blessing.

Figure 15. Mahārāj jī doing āratī. Photo by Robyn Beeche.

After the āratī, rituals continue, including offering Rādhāramaṇa a small mirror to see himself, so that he can more fully enjoy the fine adornment his loving devotees have arranged for him. After this darśana is complete and the curtains have closed, *prasāda* (a gift of food from the deity to his devotees) consisting of the tulasī leaves that have been at Rādhāramaṇa's feet is offered to those who approach the platform with hands raised to receive it. Devotees will put a leaf or two in their mouths to savor the flavor. During Mahārāj jī's sevā, the devotees are also offered a more elaborate prasāda of cut-up fruits and various sweets made of sugar and flour fried in ghi—especially the sticky mass called *halva* and the small sweet balls called *laddus,* the favorite food of the child Krishna.

Throughout the day, Krishna's activities are supported by the service of the priests and the thoughts or imaginative participation of the devotees. When the doors of the inner sanctum are open, the neighbors of Rādhāramaṇa, as well as Mahārāj jī's devotees, are present. Even when they are closed, during most of the day a few people are around in the courtyard—neighbors or visitors who come to this temple during a pilgrimage to Vrindaban. As part of Mahārāj jī's sevā, music is almost always being played and kīrtanas are being sung in the temple, and many more people than usual are around.

At noon, the āratī called *rāja bhoga* is offered; it is the same ritual as śṛṅgāra āratī, and afterward tulasī leaves are offered as prasāda. Then the temple is closed, and the priests leave. The devotees go off for lunch and a rest, and Krishna also eats and rests—though he is known to slip away during the afternoon to tryst with his beloved Rādhā.

In the early evening, the doors of the temple open again, and after some time there is another dhūpa āratī. As the evening goes on and people are free from their day's work, they come to the temple from all over Vrindaban; there are more than usual during Mahārāj jī's sevā, drawn by news of Rādhāramaṇa's gorgeous appearance and the special music that is played in his honor. The doors of the sanctum are left open, and there is a prolonged darśana (*utthāpana*), with no āratī, before the major āratī of the evening, *sandhyā āratī;* this ritual is again the same as śṛṅgāra āratī. By this time, the temple is quite crowded, and when prasāda is given out, a frenzy, a madness of grasping hands reach for the sweets that are dropped into each one. The crush—common in some temples, especially the very popular temple of Bāṅke Bihārī—is quite extraordinary in this quiet temple of Rādhāramaṇa.

The evening's entertainment of Krishna and his devotees—which during Mahārāj jī's sevā includes music, kīrtanas, and sometimes dance—is interspersed with other darśanas. *Aulāī darśana*, which is announced outside the temple by a watchman but not by the bell, precedes *bhoga āratī*, which again is announced by voice, not the bell. Then, after more chanting of the kīrtanas, the day's activities come to an end with *śayana āratī,* around 9:00 in the evening. As for maṅgala āratī in the morning, Rādhāramaṇa is in his nightclothes. The ritual is similar to that of maṅgala āratī, but now the bell and the gong are silent, the kīrtanas are sung softly. On evenings when Mahārāj jī's sevā is not on, one of the Gosvāmīs of Rādhāramaṇa Gherā plays a sweet melody on the flute as he stands before the deity, and quietly the doors are closed, and the curtains drawn for the night. Behind the closed doors, Rādhāramaṇa is laid to sleep, with an earthen pitcher of water and a plate of laddus beside him, lest he be thirsty or hungry at night. But it is known, of course, that once the lights are out, he leaves the temple to meet his beloved Rādhā until he must return for his devotees' darśana at the beginning of a new day.

Other Offerings to Rādhāramaṇa during Sevā

Mahārāj jī's sevā is envisioned to create and offer for Krishna's enjoyment the best that the arts of Vrindaban can provide, for the inducement and enhancement of bliss (*ānanda*). The temple itself, then, is during this period a continuously changing work of art. Each day, decorations in the courtyard, and especially on the platform before the sanctum, are elaborated. Cloth curtains and garlands are hung, and cut-out wooden figures of the women attendants of the divine couple—the sakhīs, whose love provides a model for all devotees—are fastened around the balcony. The bright colors of the courtyard are enhanced during two of the āratīs during the day, when stylized red and yellow flags on six-foot silver poles are brought out, as well as silver-plated maces and axes, that devotees hold as they line up in two rows to form an aisle in front of the deity. The elements of royal display (and especially Indian film images of royal display) are striking (Figure 16).

On the platform in front of the sanctum, which is normally undecorated except on festival days—and then chiefly with curtains and garlands—a succession of frame façades (*baṅgalās*) are constructed each day and assembled during the afternoon siesta time when the temple is closed. They are first revealed at the āratī at about 5:00 P.M. each day. In the summer, the baṅgalās are breathtaking filigrees of flowers strung on threads that are interlaced to make lattice walls two and three stories high. In winter, they are made with elaborate designs of dried fruits and nuts or colored paper appliqués in patterns of increasing complexity day by day. They are changed every day in the summer, every two or three days in the winter, and every few days the curtains that line the platform and the back of the inner sanctuary are also changed—red and pink and yellow and blue and green and white, in various stunning combinations. The curtains are generally plain cloth but may be embroidered or appliquéd—never printed. In the niches of the baṅgalās stand small figures of the attending sakhīs.

Toward the end of Mahārāj jī's sevā in the summer of 1997, some of the baṅgalās were, for the first time, constructed to represent specific scenes. The first was a depiction of the famous Krishna līlā when he

Figure 16. Devotees in attendance at Rādhārmaṇa temple during Mahārāj jī's sevā, December 1994.

stole the clothes of the gopīs bathing in the Yamunā. For the darśana, Rādhā and Krishna were ensconced in a bower of branches and leaves, so that they appeared to be perched in a tree. The "stolen clothes" were draped in the branches, and the gopīs were in a "pond" at the deities' feet. Another baṅgalā depicted the beautiful summer pavilion at Kusum Sarovar, near Mount Govardhana. The patterns on the "walls" were made entirely of small white flower buds sewn onto a pale green background. (It took four days to make and was kept fresh by immersion of the completed sections in water.)

Complementing this feast for the eyes were the sounds filling—one might say creating—this sacred space. Normally kīrtanas are sung before maṅgala āratī in the early morning, and there is temple singing in the evening before sandhyā āratī. The gathered devotees often sing spontaneously, especially after āratī; and often a flute is played as Krishna is put to bed. The music is played or sung with love and devotion, but with limited resources. Again, Mahārāj jī elaborated on the possibilities for musical celebration in what seemed to be every possible way.

At the outer entrance to Rādhāramaṇa Gherā were placed a drummer and a player of the *śahnāī* (a reed instrument similar to an oboe). On a small platform just outside the temple, next to the door, another śahnāī player and *nagāḍā* (drum) player were stationed during the daytime darśanas.

When the reading of the *Bhāgavata* was finished, at about 9:30 in the morning, singing began in the portico facing the deity's sanctum—dhrupada and *samāja kīrtana* temple singing—for about an hour.[12] One of the two chief singers was the master teacher of the dhrupada school at Jaisingh Ghera, the other is a professional in the sense that he makes his living from music, but he is a traditional musician whose singing is part of his own devotional practice. These two were sometimes joined by talented devotees of Mahārāj jī, who vied for a chance to sing or play. Mahārāj jī, though usually behind the curtain on the deity's platform during the singing, was always aware of what was going on, and when a raga inappropriate for the time of day was sung, he came out in front of the curtain and admonished the singer to select an appropriate one.

After the musicians finished, kīrtanas were sung in the central courtyard, before the deity. The kīrtana chanters came from Bengal or, from 1996 on, from among the villagers from Orissa with whom Mahārāj jī had been working. The energy of their chanting and the fervor of their devotion seemed to fill the temple to bursting until the āratī at midday.

The temple was closed in the afternoon, until shortly before the first evening worship. Then there was another musical offering in the evening, followed by another kīrtana until Krishna's bedtime.

During sandhyā āratī, a still more intense sound was created. In addition to the usual bells and gongs, the kīrtana singers joined in with their exuberant chants of praise. Added to this was the piercing sound of two great semicircular horns blown by devotees at the back of the temple. A big drum with a shrill, rattling sound was enthusiastically beaten on one of the porticos, and a gong pounded with all his strength by a small boy on the portico opposite it. Six eight-inch bells were hung on a framework and rung as hard and fast as they could be, often by children; finally, a conch shell, its clear sound audible only to those nearest it, was blown in the back. One could not imagine what further could be offered to the ears of Rādhāramaṇa jī. Except silence.

To offerings of sight and sound, there was added food. Cooking the deity's meals is normally the duty of four Gosvāmis at a time, two in the kitchen and two to serve the deity. For Mahārāj jī's sevā, they are assisted by a professional cook—a devotee who has taken dīkṣā from Mahārāj jī—who can prepare the fried food offered to Rādhāramaṇa, and by other Gosvāmīs who prepare the boiled rice and other boiled food. Only initiates who have touched the feet of Rādhāramaṇa can prepare the unfried food. All Rādhāramaṇa's food is cooked on a fire that has been kept burning since the time of Gopāla Bhaṭṭa in a ten-foot-long fire pit in the old temple behind the present one, and this fire is also used to light the flames that are offered in āratī and the coals that are placed in a brazier in front of his throne on the coldest mornings and evenings.

Once the food is offered to the deity, it is distributed in the way customary to this temple: one portion is given to each of the Gosvāmīs who serve in the kitchen that day; one portion to the accountant-storekeeper, one to the keeper of Gopāla Bhaṭṭa's shrine; in this case, baskets of food are given or carried to various devotees and others Mahārāj jī wishes to honor. In addition, four portions always go to what is called the *mālā*. This again is a system of rotation—each household that does a separate sevā of Rādhāramaṇa in turn receives four portions of the prasāda, as long as the head of the household is in town to receive it. The night before it is his turn, a temple servant goes to his house to inform him, and he must go to maṅgala āratī the next morning if he wishes to receive his portion that evening. If he is away, his share goes to the next person on the list. If someone is away for a full year, he can claim his portion when he returns, displacing the person whose turn it normally would have been that day.

Prasāda for the throng of devotees takes two forms: tulasī leaves that have been offered in great handfuls to the deity during āratī, and sugar, flour, and ghi in various forms—mostly halva and laddus—that are dropped by the Gosvāmīs standing on the platform before the deity into the beseeching hands of milling devotees after the mid-morning and mid-evening āratīs.

For the morning of the fourth day of the sevā in 1994, Mahārāj jī arranged a special event, a breakfast of 156 kinds of food to be prepared for Rādhāramaṇa; never before had this been done, he said. During the night before, a very elaborate baṅgalā was prepared by the baṅgalā makers, who stayed up all night, but it was hidden by white cloths draped over it at maṅgala āratī. During the morning, a curtain was drawn across the front of the platform, and all morning long baskets of food were brought in and arranged on the platform behind the curtain. There were no further darśanas during the morning; in fact, no one could approach or touch the platform while Rādhāramaṇa enjoyed his breakfast—it had become space as sacred as the inner sanctum. In the afternoon, the baskets were removed from the platform and arranged in the three porticos around the courtyard. Three large paintings depicting the sakhīs (attendants) preparing food and serving Krishna and his friends had been commissioned from the same artist who did the painting of the black bee at Bhramara ghat. One painting was now hung at the rear of each portico, and when the baskets of food were piled in front, the effect was surprisingly realistic. The food was divided by type: fruits and nuts were piled on the south portico, sweets on the east facing the sanctum, and "salty" dishes, mostly fried, on the north. Small signs with appropriate texts describing Krishna's food were propped up among the baskets.

That evening, the temple was even more packed than usual, and the crush was so great that people had to be admitted in shifts. The display was held over until the next morning "by popular demand." Then all the food—some five hundred baskets of it—was carried to Jaisingh Ghera, whence it was distributed throughout Vrindaban as a token of respect to various people. Shrivatsa's wife, Sandhyā, helped by some of the devotees, organized this major operation.

One final element in the service remains to be mentioned: light. In addition to the lighted tapers offered during āratī, and the small wicks offered by women in the morning and throughout the day, each day during Mahārāj jī's sevā about fifty small ghi lamps were lighted each evening on the front of the platform before the deity by the devotees who had had a pūjā performed for them that day.

Besides his allotted times for sevā every two years, Mahārāj jī is often invited to perform the elaborate ceremonies connected with *abhiṣeka*, the ritual bathing of Rādhāramaṇa twice a year, on the day of his appearance and on the day of Krishna's birth, Janmāṣṭamī. This is no simple bath. One hundred and eight substances are prepared and poured over him, including enormous quantities of milk, which flows for several hours in a stream from ever-renewed conch shells of liquid. Mahārāj jī himself collects and prepares the various herbs and mixtures that are involved. While the liquids are being poured, Mahārāj jī is saying the appropriate mantras and frequently instructs younger priests on the proper procedures.

Because abhiṣeka is a very complicated ceremony, there are often discussions among the many Gosvāmīs who participate. To do a ritual properly does not mean to do it as if it had been rehearsed many times and could proceed like clockwork. Discussions, even arguments, do not invalidate its efficacy, so long as in the end things are done properly and in the right order.

Rādhāramaṇa is not the only temple in which Mahārāj jī and his family are closely involved. Just down the street from Rādhāramaṇa is a small temple, Gokulānanda, for which Mahārāj jī and his family accepted responsibility in 1974, when the family caring for it died out.[13] A priest tends the deities (there are five in the sanctum) except on special occasions, when one of the Goswamis does the pūjā.

In addition, the priest of Gokulānanda walks to Jaisingh Ghera every morning and evening carrying a brass tray with items for āratī (and a cane under his arm to chase monkeys). He does pūjā at the family's shrine where Mātā jī used to do much of the sevā and, since the appearance of the black bee, at the shrine on Bharamara ghat. (Sevā at the family's shrine during the rest of the day is done by the family.) The priest at Gokulānanda is also an excellent cook, who prepares a large feast for Krishna on Annakūṭa, the day after Dīpāvalī (Dīvālī) in the fall; all the neighbors come to sit in the temple's courtyard and enjoy the prasāda.

In addition, Mahārāj jī and Shrivatsa in 1998 assumed responsibility for the shrine of Vinodīlāla in Jaipur, one of the deities that was originally in Gokulānanda temple before it had to leave in the eighteenth century.[14] As with Gokulānanda, the family serving it had died out and it was not being properly cared for, so the Goswamis arranged to become the custodians.

Also in Jaipur is the great temple of Govindadeva, whose temple in Vrindaban, before the deity's departure, had been the center of the town. Mahārāj jī has a close relationship with the Gosvāmīs who serve Govindadeva, and in 1995 he was in charge of organizing a great celebration there. That is the next story.

SIX

GOVINDADEVA TEMPLE

A Festival of Devotion

In about 1534, about twenty years after Śrī Caitanya came to Vrindaban, tradition has it that the foremost of the Six Gosvāmīs he had sent to Vrindaban, Rūpa Gosvāmī, noticed a cow shedding her milk on a hillside. This is the hill that is considered the *yogapīṭha*, the place of Rādhā and Krishna's ultimate union, and the spiritual center of Vrindaban. Rūpa dug into the hillside at that spot and unearthed the black stone figure of Govindadeva—Krishna in his aspect as the protector of cows, Krishna the flute player, Krishna the *rasika* or enjoyer of the flavor of life, whose presence in Vrindaban fulfills the need of divinity to enjoy his own sweetness to the fullest.

When Śrī Caitanya heard of the find, he identified it as one of the images in Vrindaban that had been made under the aegis of Krishna's grandson, the other three being Madanamohana, Gopīnātha, and Vinodīlāla. In the course of time, these images had been buried. Now that the image of Govindadeva was recovered, a small brick temple was immediately built for it, and it attracted patronage from Rājput chiefs, including the royal house of Āmera.

It is an accepted part of the traditional history of the area that when, in 1571, the crown prince of Āmera, Māna Siṃha (Man Singh)—a close friend of the Mughal emperor Akbar—undertook to fight the forces of the Rājput state of Mevāra, he vowed that if he was successful he would build a great temple for Govindadeva in Vrindaban. He was successful, and he did. The temple was completed in 1590. It was a magnificent structure, said to be the largest single building serving as a

Hindu temple in all India. Its outstanding feature was the large interior vaulted space, suitable for the devotional kīrtana and performance of rāsalīlās that were part of Caitanyaite practice.[1]

Śrī Govindadeva was able to enjoy his new home for less than a century before he had to leave for safer quarters. During the reign of the last of the great Mughals, Akbar's great-grandson Aurangzeb, political turmoil convulsed the empire, and by Aurangzeb's order the great Hindu temples at Varanasi and—very close to home—Mathura were razed. The Gosvāmīs of Vrindaban feared for the safety of the images under their care and escorted most of them to safer territory to the west, still under Rājput control.

Govindadeva went first to the village of Rādhākuṇḍa, near the sacred Mount Govardhana a few miles west of Vrindaban, where for two years he stayed in a *havelī*-style temple built to look exactly like a residence.[2] From Rādhākuṇḍa, the deity was moved to the towns of Kāmāṅ, Govindagaḍha, Khavā, and Govindapurā, each off the imperial highway and successively farther into Hindu-controlled territory. In 1713, forty-three years after leaving Vrindaban, the deity was housed in a temple built for him at the base of the escarpment protecting the approach to Āmera fort, which was named Kanaka Vṛndāvana, Golden Vrindaban. Its position on the open plain and its spacious, airy architecture spoke of the confidence of the ruler of Āmera, Savāī Jayasiṃha (Jaisingh), that the deity was in no danger there from hostile forces.

Meanwhile, Savāī Jayasiṃha—he who established Jaisingh Ghera—was beginning construction of the new capital city he had designed, to be named Jaipur (Jayapura). Two years after Govindadeva was established in Kanaka Vṛndāvana, the deity was moved to a building in the newly laid-out gardens behind the site of the royal palace in Jaipur, until his permanent home, a new temple in those gardens, was completed. Jaipur was laid out on a grid or mandala of nine squares, with the palace complex in the central square: a long mall running north-south with Jaya Siṃha's palace at one end (and just beyond it, the *jantar mantar* for astronomical observations); in the middle, a temple to house Govindadeva; and behind that to the north, gardens with fountains and walkways, ending in a large square "tank" or pond (see plan, Figure 17).[3] Jaya Siṃha's palace was named Candra Mahala (Moon Palace), and Govindadeva's temple was named Sūrya Mahala (Sun Palace).

There continued to be close links between the temples of Govindadeva in Vrindaban and Jaipur, however, and the rulers of Āmera and Jaipur continued to support the guardians of the Vrindaban temple until sometime in the 1720s. Thereafter, the Vrindaban temple seems to

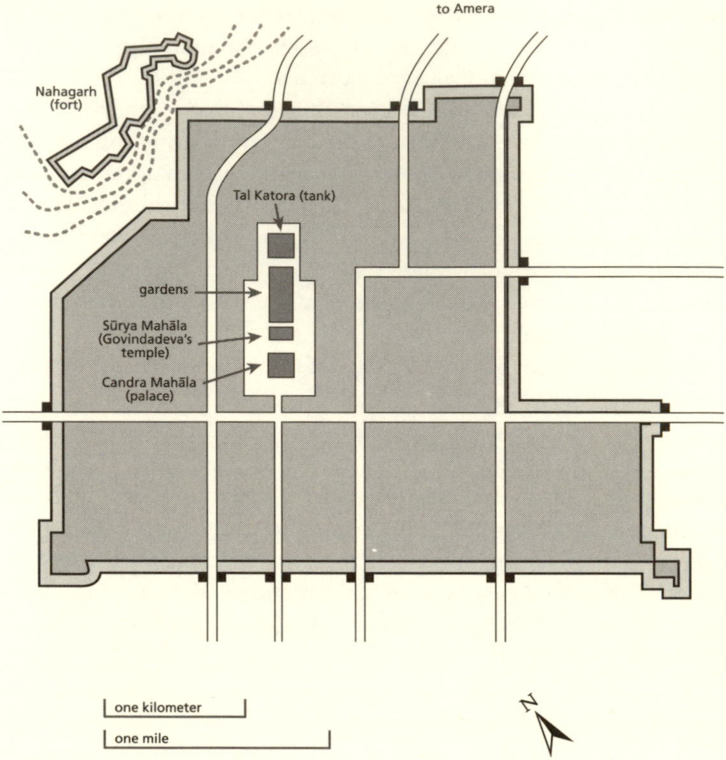

Figure 17. Plan of Jaipur maṇḍala. Drawing by Nat Case.

have fallen on hard times, and by the 1870s it was on the verge of collapse. It was propped up and repaired by the energetic British district collector of Mathura in the 1870s, Frederic Salmon Growse, and from then on was one of the many places of pilgrimage in this town that, as Vaiṣṇava merchants prospered and transportation improved in the nineteenth century, became a major center of pilgrim traffic.[4]

In Jaipur, Sūrya Mahala was built, in fact, to be the home of Jaipur's ruler. When Govindadeva was installed in it in 1727, the rāja declared that Govindadeva jī was thenceforth the ruler of the state of Āmera and Jaipur and that he himself was only the chief minister of the deity. The overt reason given was Savāī Jayasiṃha's great, and indubitable, devotion to the deity. More pragmatic reasons suggested by Shrivatsa Goswami include his wish to keep the image in Jaipur despite the Vrindaban Gosvāmīs' repeated requests that it be returned, and the value of the deity's presence in overawing the fractious subchiefs of Rajasthan. After Jayasiṃha installed the deity in Sūrya Mahala, he performed an *aśvamedha yajña* in Govindadeva's name. This is the Vedic ritual horse sacrifice, whereby a ruler lets a horse roam freely for a year and claims all the territory covered by the horse as his own. It was a bold assertion of Govindadeva's power (and that of Jaipur), one that had not been practiced since ancient times. That it was done in the deity's name would have helped defuse the jealousy of those on whom this power impinged.[5]

Jayasiṃha's successors continued the tradition of Govindadeva's rulership until Rajasthan joined the Indian Union after Independence. The deity is still regarded as the king of Jaipur by the people of the city and surrounding countryside, and they offer him intense devotion.

Govindadeva's temple in Jaipur looks in many ways like the audience hall of a ruler of the Mughal period. Far from being sequestered in a cavelike, pillared hall, like many deities, or ensconced within a courtyard house, he stands virtually in the open, at the front of a small building surrounded on three sides by a covered passageway through which the devotees can walk as they circumambulate. He looks out toward the rāja's palace to the south, across a low marble platform that is separated from the public space by a sturdy brass rail, and whose roof is supported by massive marble pillars. The ceiling of this space and the outer walls of the deity's room are pink stucco painted with delicate drawings. The priests and a few privileged devotees may go up on the marble platform; all others crowd up to the brass rail, standing, until recently, under the sun or stars for their darśana of the deity.

During the 1990s, a new pavilion (*ārādhana maṇḍapa*) was built over the open space in front of the temple. Designed to replicate the workmanship of the eighteenth-century building, it was both expensive and time-consuming to construct. By 1995, though still incomplete, this new pavilion was sufficiently finished to be dedicated, and Mahārāj jī was asked to come from Vrindaban to organize a monthlong celebration of the event. There have long been ties between Mahārāj jī and the devotees of Govindadeva in Jaipur, and his seven-day discourses in the temple, given every year since the 1960s, have always attracted a large audience. This celebration was an extension of the annual event.

The temple grounds were decorated for the occasion to establish a festival air. Banners were hung, a brightly colored gateway was constructed of cloth stretched on a framework, the main path to the temple was lined with boards painted with auspicious signs and pictures of overflowing pots of greens, a fire shrine was built, a low wall at the back of the new pavilion was decorated with colored cloth, and a stage and enormous tent (*paṇḍāla*) were constructed to the west of the temple, for performances.

The major opening event was to be a recitation of the entire *Bhāgavata Purāṇa* by 108 brahmans, invited to come for the occasion from all over India. It was to take seven days, about five hours a day. Before they began, the brahmans gathered at the back of the new pavilion, where one by one they sat in front of Mahārāj jī, who washed their feet as a token of humble respect, assisted by his sons. Many of the brahmans, especially the oldest ones, were extremely moved by the service rendered to them, and some tried to refuse. But eventually all went through the ritual and received the deep yellow cloths that they were to wear throughout the reading.

Then they were seated on the ground at rows of low benches, also covered with deep yellow cloth. Each was given a copy of the *Bhāgavata Purāṇa* and small water pots with diminutive spoons, which they were to use to wet their mouths during the recitation; they arrived in a pure state, having bathed after sleeping, and could not eat or drink again until the day's reading was over. Each was individually given offerings of tulasī leaves, flower blossoms, money, fruits, and sweets, all handed out by men of the Goswami family and a few devotees. A garland was placed on each copy of the text, and then Mahārāj jī himself placed them around the readers' necks and put a tilaka, mark of sandalwood paste, on each one's forehead. This ritual, honoring both the text and the readers, was repeated each morning before the reading.

The reading began with the ritual blessing, spoken by all in unison, invoking the various deities whose blessing was sought. One brahman led the invocation and then the reading, speaking into a microphone. Not only did the sound echo through the temple and the grounds around it but loudspeakers also carried it outside the temple, and the words could be heard throughout the neighborhood. The sun streamed in on the 108 brahmans, and the brilliant yellow of their cloths against the multicolored decorations on the wall behind them contrasted with the vivid reds, pinks, purples, and blues of the clothes of the women who crowded in the temple and along the wall behind them to look and to listen. Few could understand the Sanskrit text, but all felt the power of the sound. Each day, the readings continued from about seven in the morning until one or two o'clock, with breaks only during the regular worship services in the temple, for the sound of the bells and gongs during āratī would have drowned out the sound of the readings.

The reading of the text was completed in seven days, but two more days were taken to read aloud once again the tenth canto of the *Bhāgavata*

Purāṇa, the portion dealing specifically with the life of Krishna. These readings accompanied the performance of a fire sacrifice by some of the brahmans. For this sacrifice, a special building had been constructed south of the walkway leading to the temple: a square wooden building with open sides on a concrete platform, with an alter on the east and a fire pit in the center. It was built according to the very exact requirements of *vāstu śāstra*, the traditional "building codes" that establish auspicious directions, natural features, the arrangement of the component elements of a building, and its placement on the site. On the evening before the sacrifice began, the building was consecrated by Shrivatsa Goswami with his wife, Sandhyā, and the eldest son of the chief priest of Govindadeva temple with his wife, as the ritual sacrificers. The two-day sacrifice itself was in part conducted by these four and in part by brahmans from among the *Bhāgavata* readers.

Those who performed the sacrifice sat around the fire pit, while one priest read aloud the tenth canto, verse (*śloka*) by verse. At the end of each verse, the word *svāhā* was uttered while the sacrificers put a ladleful of ghi and some sesame into the fire. Because the sides of the building were open, onlookers could stand outside, watching.

The fire sacrifice, like all Vedic rituals, is considered a very high, very powerful ritual, and the requirements for purity and correct procedures are complex and stringent. Because in the present age it is virtually impossible to fulfill all these requirements exactly, Mahārāj jī does not ordinarily conduct or encourage this sacrifice. Instead, he performs a tulasī sacrifice to mark the end of his discourses on the *Bhāgavata*. The requirements of this ritual are much less rigorous, and all devotees can participate in it, thus making it more suitable for popular devotion in the present age.

During the week when the *Bhāgavata Purāṇa* was being recited, Mahārāj jī spoke for two to three hours every afternoon on themes from the text—a modified seven-day discourse. He sat on a dais to the west side of the new pavilion, facing the crowd that would gather there for darśana of the deity. The number of people who came to hear him usually started at about a thousand and doubled or tripled by the time he finished each day. They came also for evening worship at the temple, for Mahārāj jī spoke right up to the time that the doors to Govindadeva's sanctum were opened—and toward the end of the week, the opening was often delayed while he finished speaking. When some of those in the gathering crowd became restless or simply talked among themselves—there is no sense among worshipers that silence is to be maintained in the temple—Mahārāj jī spoke strongly, telling them to be quiet and listen, as this also was worship of Govindadeva that was being conducted. He commanded great respect from the people of Jaipur, and in general they followed his directions.

Each morning throughout the festival, Mahārāj jī conducted one, two, or more special pūjās for individuals among his devotees who requested them. Each individual for whom a pūjā was performed was assessed one gold sovereign, worth four thousand rupees or, at the current exchange rate, about $125. During the pūjās, conducted in the space within the brass railings, the crowd continued to stand for darśana of the deity, and to fling their offerings into the area—bananas, pomegranates, apples, water chestnuts, sweet potatoes, coins, and even coconuts, the items often hitting those standing on the platform. Those who stood there before the presence of the deity could feel very concretely the enthusiasm of the crowd on one side, as well as a palpable sense of energy emanating from the deity.[6]

At some time each day—morning, afternoon, or evening, depending on the rest of the schedule—a circle of Mahārāj jī's devotees and a crowd of perhaps a couple of hundred others gathered to chant sādhānikā hymns (like those sung during the days of mourning for Mātā jī), printed in booklets and distributed to the crowd; these were usually led by Mahārāj jī's younger son, Veṇu Gopāla.

After the week-long reading of the *Bhāgavata Purāṇa* had set the tone of the festivities, the focus of events shifted to evening performances. The first performance to be presented on the temporary stage built beside the temple was by the national award-winning dancer Sonal Mansingh. It was before her that the black bee had first appeared in Vrindaban. On the next three nights, there were performances of rāsalīlās by members of the Vrindaban troupe regularly patronized by Mahārāj jī, the Svāmī Fatehkṛṣṇa Rāsmaṇḍali. The first two rāsalīlās had been written especially for this celebration; they told the story of the original manifestation of Govindadeva, his rediscovery by Rūpa Gosvāmī, the role of Caitanya in inspiring his establishment in a new temple, and his journey to Jaipur. The third rāsalīlā, on the night of the full moon of the month of Karttika (a month especially associated with Krishna), was the often-performed līlā of the great circle dance (*mahārāsa*), when Krishna fulfills the desires of the gopīs by multiplying himself and dancing with each one under the full moon.

After this, four evenings were devoted to a "conference" on dharma. Each evening, half a dozen to a dozen invited religious and academic authorities sat on the stage to speak on the theme. It was most unusual to see these luminaries in the religious realm of India sitting on a platform unaccompanied by the paraphernalia or the retinue with which they usually appear, and their willingness to appear in such a format was evidence of their respect for Mahārāj jī and Shrivatsa. Managing these visiting dignitaries was a challenge, for the protocol among the many religious leaders of various sects, who have adopted or been accorded grandiloquent titles, is both subtle and crucial to the continuing relations among them. Such civilities as meeting people's trains and planes, providing accommodations and transportation, and seating people at such an event, not to mention arranging the order in which they were to speak, were among the details to which the Goswamis paid constant and personal attention during the celebration.

On two subsequent evenings, there were dance performances choreographed to music written by Premlata Sharma, the distinguished musicologist from Varanasi, by two different dance troupes, one the company of Śrīmatī Kumudanī Lākhīa-Kadamba of Ahmedabad, the other that of Professor Chandrasekhara-Nṛtyaśrī of Baroda. These troupes specialize in interpreting traditional themes and dance styles in innovative idioms. It should be emphasized that the focus of all the performers at this festival was expected to be not so much display of their own talents as worship of Govindadeva.

A style of rāsalīlā quite different from that of the Vrindaban troupe was presented on two evenings by a troupe of men from Calcutta, the Hāvḍā Samāja, who presented both a Krishna līlā and a Caitanya līlā. The troupe was started in the 1930s; the members devote their spare time outside their jobs in banks, offices, and elsewhere to this form of devotion, which they have maintained as a family and community tradition. The man who these days plays the role of Nityānanda, closest associate of Caitanya, for example, is the son and grandson of men who previously took that role. To eyes accustomed to seeing young boys in these līlās, it is startling to see grown men, some fairly heavy, play these same parts (Figure 18). But their emotional conviction (*bhāva*) and their expert acting in a slow, kabuki-like dramatic style on a bare stage have a unique effectiveness.

Finally, the preparations and preliminaries complete, the time arrived for the aṣṭayāma līlā, the eight-day presentation of the life of Krishna. Behind the scenes—or, literally, on the veranda around a circular room that served as Shrivatsa's office during the celebration—finishing touches were put on the costumes and props. Virtually all the costumes were made especially for this production, designed by Shrivatsa's wife, Sandhyā, and assembled and sewn under her personal care. On the afternoon of the last day before the opening performance, large boxes arrived from

Varanasi, laden with magnificent golden and bejeweled ornaments for Krishna and Rādhā and the other participants.

The adornment of the actors embodies the visualization of divinity in the active imagination of the devotee, and the imagination of those creating the costumes and adornment is fed by a whole tradition of poetry, painting, and theater, which have their roots, ultimately, in the verses of the *Bhāgavata Purāṇa*. Describing Krishna's beauty, the *Bhāgavata Purāṇa* several times says that as the cowherd women waited for him to return to the village in the evening, they could see Krishna in their minds' eye:

> On his head was a peacock feather and in his ears were earrings of yellow flowers; he was wearing a yellow silk cloth, and around his neck hung a garland of five kinds of fragrant flowers. What a beautiful costume for the most exalted actor, playing on a colorful stage! He filled the holes of his flute with the nectar of his lips. (X.21.5)

Indeed, the adornment of Krishna, Rādhā, the sakhīs, the cowherd men, and all the individual characters is a focus of loving attention and great labor during the preparation for the līlās. Just as the adornment of Rādhāramaṇa is essential to darśana in the temple, the adornment of the players in the drama is vital in a creation that engages all the senses, enabling those present to participate in the divine.

During the evening before the first performance, the stage was being prepared to create a forest grove, and no one was permitted behind the curtain but the baṅgalā makers who were working on it. This was not simply the preparation of a stage set, after all, but the preparation of a "divine comedy." To see it in an unfinished state would be to profane it.

All the stage settings were simple. There were two basic scenes during the līlā: forest and palace; other action took place in front of the curtain. The scene throughout the performance of the first night was a forest bower, a scene in harmony with the poetry being sung; the stage was designed to enhance the imagination, stimulated by the music and poetry, not overwhelm it. Fresh flowers and leaves were tied into place in the hours before the performance. Cut trees and branches were set in the background and placed about the stage; for many scenes, they were hung with a multitude of flowers, and sometimes papier-mâché birds were perched on them.

The indoor scenes of the aṣṭayāma līlā suggested a palace, and yet the palace of the chief of cowherds who were said to have no permanent home. The requirements of theater and scripture came together in hangings in the shape of pillared arches, brilliant red and embroidered

Figure 18. Krishna as played by a member of the Hāvḍā Samāja, Calcutta. Jaipur, November 1995. Photo by Robyn Beeche.

with sequins and "gems." Their lushness signified royalty and recalled miniature paintings of royal palaces, but their fluidity—they moved whenever someone passed them—retained the ambiguity as to whether the "palace" was an encampment. Virtually the only other props for the indoor scenes were two thrones that appeared throughout the performances (and sometimes in the outdoor scenes as well). They were wooden seats that held two people comfortably. One was covered in royal blue, the back decorated with a peacock pattern made of small golden pieces tacked in place; the arms were also decorated with a golden pattern. The other seat was covered in a brilliant red cloth and decorated with a tree, each golden leaf individually tacked in place.

The scripts of the aṣṭayāma līlās performed under Mahārāj jī's direction were written by him. The underlying text for the Krishna līlā was the *Govindalīlāmṛta* (Ambrosia of the Sport of Govinda), a long poem written by Kṛṣṇadāsa Kavirāja in the sixteenth century.[7] The words for the script came almost entirely from the body of poetry and song that has been created continuously since the sixteenth century, in Vraja and Bengal, which constitutes the fabric of the culture of Vraja.

The actors, though young, were talented, trained, and experienced in the art of the rāsalīlā. In addition to rehearsing the scripts and songs on their own, they met several times to rehearse with Mahārāj jī. The aim was for the actors to produce a spontaneous performance, not necessarily a polished one. Their talent, enthusiasm, and verve carried the performance. Their task was made somewhat easier both by the fact that much of the poetry being sung was familiar and by the form of the drama, in which virtually all the lines were said twice; Svāmī Fatehkṛṣṇa, the troupe's director, who stood at a lectern at one side of the stage playing a harmonium, chanted all the lines. If he was acting as narrator or chorus, he chanted each line twice. If there was action on stage, either he chanted the line and the actor echoed him, or vice versa. The second recitation was the same as the first; there was no translation of the Sanskrit, Bengali, or Braj bhāṣā, the Vraja dialect of Hindi, into standard Hindi. The result was to slow the action and give the words themselves priority; if the audience missed the words the first time, it had a chance to catch them the second. But the poetry was known by heart to much of the audience, in any case, and the story line was familiar. The audience did not depend on catching every word to enter into the drama.

Although I focus in the following two chapters on the aṣṭayāma līlās that celebrated the eternal life of Krishna—the performances when the black bee appeared in 1992, and the performances in Jaipur in 1996—the first aṣṭayāma līlā staged by Mahārāj jī, in 1989, cast Caitanya Mahāprabhu as protagonist.[8] The hagiography of Caitanya, as we have seen, echoes the stories of Krishna's childhood, and the body of stories and poetry about Caitanya often confounds the two manifestations of the deity. The parallels are drawn in three main ways: Caitanya, as an avatar of Krishna and Rādhā combined, often acts as Krishna did; the people historically connected with him are envisioned as assuming roles similar to those of the family and associates of Krishna; and Caitanya often envisions Krishna's līlās, which are then enacted as part of his story. The tradition makes much of Caitanya's mother and his wife, whom he left to become a sannyāsī, and there are echoes in this of Krishna leaving Rādhā and the gopīs. Caitanya's immediate circle of disciples were all male, but they all aspired to have the consciousness of the sakhīs, the female companions of the divine couple. And always one is aware that when Caitanya was "seized" by the divine, he was seized by both Krishna and Rādhā. A Caitanya līlā is therefore even richer than a Krishna līlā in the multiplicity of personae embodied in the protagonist and in the echoes of Purāṇic, poetic, and historical referents.

As Shrivatsa Goswami explains the relationship between the Caitanya and Krishna līlās, however, the connection between them goes much deeper than this similarity of themes, into historical indebtedness and even into ontology, illuminating the nature of existence.[9] It was through Caitanya's memory of Krishna's līlās and his identification of their locales, witnessed by his followers, that the custom developed of staging the Krishna līlās in temples. This custom evolved into the present practice of staging rāsalīlās both on the geographical sites of their occurrence during the annual vana yātrā pilgrimage and on stage. Mahārāj jī's staging of the aṣṭayāma līlās grew out of this rāsalīlā tradition and drew, as well, on the literary development of the story of the relationship between Rādhā and Krishna begun in Jayadeva's *Gītagovinda* and developed in Kṛṣṇadāsa Kavirāja's *Govindalīlāmṛtam*.

In understanding the meaning of the staged aṣṭayāma līlās, one starts with the premise that the eternal līlās of Krishna and Rādhā exist, just as the visible world exists, though they may or may not be seen by humans. They also exist in the "theater of memory" of those who have known Krishna. Those who have known him suffer from his absence, just as the cowherd women suffer when he goes out to the fields with his calves. In separation, the longing for him entails a sublime enjoyment of his "taste" (*rasa*) in the theater of memory. The condition of separation thus induces a mood in which union with him can be experienced, through memory. So when Krishna left the women of Vrindaban, Uddhava and his message meant nothing to them; they longed for Krishna and adored him in the theater of memory, and Uddhava was not a player on that stage. When Rādhā invoked the context of memory in which Krishna lived, then Krishna appeared to her and the other women in the form of the bee.

Caitanya, Shrivatsa continues, knew Krishna's literary form, the *Bhāgavata Purāṇa* (which Krishna had declared to be identical to himself) by virtue of his being an incarnation. The images of the *Bhāgavata* triggered Caitanya's memory, so that he "saw" the Yamunā River in any river or ocean, Mount Govardhana in every hill, and the sites of Krishna's līlās everywhere he went, and himself reenacted the līlās as he saw them. Not satisfied with the clues he found around him in Bengal or Orissa, he traveled to Vrindaban near Mathura, and there he identified and reestablished the real locations of Krishna's līlās. But his discovery and reenactment were still partial, and he inspired the Six Goswamis and other colleagues to fill in the gaps in the *Bhāgavata Purāṇa*'s record through their own study, experience, and insight, thus enlarging the theater of memory.

In 1992, Shrivatsa goes on, those who came to Bhramara ghat for the aṣṭayāma līlā were suffering from their separation from Krishna—and Caitanya—and they sought him there in the form of the *svarūpa*, the Krishna of the staged līlās. The power of the staged līlās lies in their ability to awaken, in those who are watching, Krishna's eternal līlā in the theater of memory. The aṣṭayāma līlā is the most powerful of the staged līlās in this respect, for it engages the devotee in the highest spiritual activity, the twenty-four-hour drama of remembering the eternal līlā of Krishna (*aṣṭayāma līlā smaraṇa*).

The eternal līlā is unmanifest, just as memory is unmanifest. But when all was prepared for the unmanifest to become manifest (on stage), says Shrivatsa, then Krishna appeared in the form of the black bee, the only form possible in that context. He was summoned, as an incarnation must always be summoned, by the mantras. He came so he could enjoy the enjoyment of the devotees, for the enjoyment of the divinity comes through humanity, and vice versa.

The descriptions that follow are drawn from all three productions of the aṣṭayāma līlā: the Caitanya līlā in Vrindaban in 1989, the Krishna līlā in Vrindaban in 1992 (when the black bee appeared), and the Krishna līlā in Jaipur in 1995.[10] The next two chapters take up each day's līlā in turn and first give a detailed description of the Krishna līlās—those in Vrindaban and Jaipur were quite similar—and then a summary of the Caitanya līlā for that day. Although the Caitanya līlā takes precedence chronologically and metaphysically, nevertheless it was at a Krishna līlā that the black bee appeared, and the context of its appearance is the story of this book.

SEVEN

SEEING KRISHNA

Aṣṭayāma Līlā

First Day, 3:36 A.M.

The town is dark and silent; it is three in the morning. Houses are blank behind their walls and gates, shops are shuttered. Cows and dogs are lying on the roads, asleep. But streams of people are walking through the streets and alleys, converging on the place where, for a few hours of each day for the next week, they can be in the presence of the eternal life of Krishna and his friends. Whether it is the great hall of Jaisingh Ghera in Vrindaban or the special stage and tent set up beside Govindadeva Temple in Jaipur does not matter. In this early morning darkness, the time, the preparations, and the expectation have created the occasion for darśana. People come with an excitement of anticipation that overrides their sleepiness.

Inside the hall or tent people crowd to sit as far forward as possible—men on the right facing the stage, women on the left, with an aisle between that is quickly filled with people. Everyone sits cross-legged on the rugs, crammed improbably close together, prepared to sit quietly in that position for about three hours. The crowd will appear to have covered the whole space, and yet a latecomer will be called in to join her friends—this happens most notably among the women—and where there was the slimmest space, she will insert herself while others redistribute themselves around her, accommodating inch by inch and exchanging sympathetic smiles with others nearby. Sometimes a woman who is not welcomed by the others will move in and squat, perhaps in an area roped off for family and close devotees. Requests by the ushers to move are met with a smile, a nod of agreement, and perhaps a shift of weight ever so slightly in some direction. Either the usher smiles and gives up, or really insists, in which case she wriggles back into the crowd, and the others give way. The ushers need constant vigilance, for if one is called away, instantly three or four women slip in and sit firmly in the territory he has been guarding. There is some murmur of conversation in the crowd, but there is little noise.

Meanwhile, behind the curtain of the stage, the craftsmen are scrambling to finish the scenery before the hour and minute when the show must begin. There are always last-minute adjustments, unforeseen contingencies to deal with; one of the principles of the production is spontaneity, and each enactment is a new creation. As the audience gathers in the hall or tent, in the "green room" behind the stage the players are finishing their dressing and makeup, and the baṅgala makers, who are stagehands for this production as they are scene makers for Mahārāj jī's sevā in Rādhāramaṇa, are putting the last boughs and bunches of flowers in place. At precisely 3:36, the astrologically determined moment that the new day begins, the house lights go out, and Mahārāj jī's voice is heard from behind the curtain.

In Jaipur, Mahārāj jī began by reminding everyone that the aṣṭayāma līlā is a worship of the Lord, Bhagavān, that it is a darśana of the eternal līlā that is occurring all the time, but can be seen only by those who have eyes to see it. Similarly, in 1992, when the aṣṭayāma līlā began a few hours after the first appearance of the black bee, Mahārāj jī told the gathered devotees that the events on Bhramara ghat, the coming of Uddhava and the declarations of the women's love for Krishna, were not in the imagination, they were eternal, and they go on all the time. "Yesterday we could see it, four to five hundred people had the evidence of their eyes; it would be lying to say that such a thing is not real, though we usually cannot see it." This time, he says, we will have an opportunity to see what the *ṛṣis* (Vedic seers) and sages pray for in all their austerities and cannot achieve. This is an opportunity to experience Krishna.

Then the musical leader of the troupe, the *svāmī*, begins his invocations to confirm the auspiciousness of the occasion.[1] The curtain remains down for a long time—perhaps half an hour—while he sings:

> Let us devote ourselves to the lotus feet of Govinda. . . . By touching the dust of the feet of Rādhāramaṇa all our desires will be filled. Let me touch my head to the divine dust of the lotus feet of the guru, so that I may have the enjoyment of serving Rādhā and Krishna. Let us worship

> Rūpa, Sanātana, Raghunātha, and Jīva [four of the Six Gosvāmīs], who touch the heart. Let us adore the lotus feet of Śrī Gopāla Bhaṭṭa and Raghunātha Bhaṭṭa, the source of the world's holiness. . . . Let us adore Vraja and the holy places where Rādhā and Krishna daily take their eternal enjoyment.

And so on. The poetry and the music are familiar to the audience and establish the emotional setting—the *bhāva*—for the performance.

When the curtain goes up, the stage, bathed in a pale blue, watery light, at first seems to have no one on it, other than a few musicians sitting behind the svāmī. The scene is a forest bower, encompassing a gigantic lotus blossom made of silvery strips of banana-wood pith. As our eyes become accustomed to the light, we see Rādhā and Krishna lying asleep on the lotus. This is the yogapīṭha, the center of Vrindaban and of Vraja. It is the place of the intimate union of Rādhā and Krishna.

The svāmī sings of the beauty of the scene:

> Rādhā and Krishna are sleeping within the beautiful bower of trees, and flowers grow around them.
> Sometimes they sleep, sometimes they walk about under the full moon of autumn, very happy in the cool breeze that has ended the heat of the summer sun.
> The water of the Yamunā, daughter of the sun, is sweet and cool.

They are embracing, says the poet, and sleeping; "they drink the nectar of each other's lips on the bed made of flowers." The poetry describing the beauty of the scene goes on for some time, while the divine couple continue sleeping, stirring only occasionally. What is being established is the emotional experience of *mādhurya,* the sweet taste of erotic love for Krishna, through which his nature is known by Rādhā and her attendants (*sakhīs*).

Then the svāmī sings that Vṛndādevī, the goddess of the sacred tulasī (basil, also called vṛnda) forest in whose domain the yogapīṭha stands, and through whose powers the tryst of the divine couple was possible, awakens and realizes that it is late, that her two charges should get home to their own beds. The goddess appears on stage with some of the sakhīs, and Vṛndādevī says to Lalitā, the foremost of the sakhīs: "Lalitā, let's awaken them by playing the sweet vīṇā." But the notes of the vīṇā do not awaken the divine lovers. A pair of birds come in (boys in cloaks and bird masks): "please leave this moonlit bed . . . the night is finished, the morning has come, the sun is rising, it's time to awake. . . . The cowherds are waiting for you, please go to them and fulfil their wishes . . . please go back to your palace before the people of Vraja awaken.

Leave this flowered bed." The lovers do not stir. Then two deer come in—other boys in costume—and two peacocks enter and do their dance. All the dialogue on stage is either preceded or followed by the svāmī's singing the same, or nearly the same, words; the repetition gives the audience time to absorb the words and their meaning.

By this time, perhaps an hour and a half of the performance has elapsed. The production is clearly not primarily focused on action or a story line. It is to be found in the music and the poetry, combined with the tableau, which nourish the imagination and the feelings of those who are watching. Krishna, the very essence of bliss, can be known through the evocation of bliss in the theater of memory.[2]

Now Rādhā and Krishna finally stir and sit up, and the sakhīs come to help them arrange themselves and then give them a mirror to look in; the lovers gaze at each other's beauty. The svāmī describes their beauty and their happiness, and the sakhīs come to stand near them, describing the scene to one another. The first sakhī says, "Just look—the shining of the moon, and the blue glow of the night sky, what a sight they make together!" It is an image that awakens a sense of wonder and beauty that everyone must feel in India when the luminous moon shines high and bright in the clear, dark sky. The moonlight is brilliant even when the moon is only half full, and dazzling on the night of the full moon. The moon is celebrated in poetry as a source of life, for it is associated with water. The moonbeams are thought to be liquid, and the moon controls the tides of the sea; the crescent moon worn in Śiva's hair is associated with the river Ganges that flows to earth through his locks. The dark sky and the cool night air are a relief and refreshment than can be appreciated best by those who endure for so much of the year the burning sky and scorching sun of India.

A second sakhī says, "No, friend, in my opinion they look like an entire galaxy playing with the clouds." A third sakhī says, "O friend, I don't think you are right; I say that the moon has risen from the clouds." Each of these variations on the theme carries with it memories of other songs and poems of love and devotion that enhance and enrich the audience's sense of the beauty of the scene.

A fourth sakhī contradicts them all, saying, "No, friend, we can't compare Krishna with the moon because the moon has a flaw [that is, it wanes as well as waxes], but I say that we are seeing a golden creeper twining around a black *tamāla* tree." The image evokes their loving embrace and also suggests the entire range of images that depict Rādhā and Krishna as inseparable, two aspects of the same being. It is a theme that is represented in many ways—sentimentally in song, dramatically with the two intertwined in dance, artistically in drawings of a being half Krishna and half Rādhā, theologically in the understanding of Śrī Caitanya Mahāprabhu's nature, and philosophically in the fundamental principle of Caitanyaite Vaiṣṇavism: *acintyabhedābheda*, inconceivable difference in nondifference.

Lalitā tells the others that these comparisons fail to capture the actuality of the scene. "O sakhīs, what you are describing is not enough. I will use words that actually describe what we are seeing. The incarnation of *rasa*, Śrī Krishna, and the incarnation of *bhāva*, Śrī Rādhā, are sitting together on the bed of flowers."

The root meaning of *rasa* is juice, sap, or liquid; it implies, on the one hand, essence, the essential nature of a thing, or its flavor. On the other hand, it connotes enjoyment, pleasure taken in a thing, and, more abstractly, the various tastes or sentiments that can be expressed artistically.[3] In one word, it expresses the whole aesthetic that underlies Vaiṣṇava spirituality—that whatever exists in the world should be accepted and enjoyed in its essential nature by those who live in the world. It can be understood as awareness, the active principle of one's inner life.

Bhāva also has many meanings. In Vaiṣṇava usage, it indicates a deeply felt receptivity of mind, heart, and soul toward a manifestation of the divine. It is the passive principle of inner life. So Lalitā's description of the divine lovers evokes metaphysically the play of interaction between the inseparable pairs, essence and existence, active and passive, or the subtleties of enjoyment and being enjoyed.

The complementarity of Rādhā and Krishna is the theme of the next song, which in twenty verses celebrates the mutuality of their relationship. By now Rādhā and Krishna have gotten up and, after walking a while around the stage arm in arm, are seated on a red throne to gaze at one another while the sakhīs and the svāmī sing:

> Jaya Śrī Rādhā, the maiden who enjoys rasa, and Krishna, who is the alchemist of rasa.
>
> Jaya Śrī Rādhā, whose color is pale gold, and Krishna, who is blue like a thick mass of clouds. . . .

The song is unsatisfactory in translation because the poetry lies in words that are virtual homonyms on each side of the caesura.

Then comes the food, an essential part of each day's līlā. The imagery of mutual nourishment goes to the heart of devotion, so considerable time and attention are given to the foods prepared and served to the deities, whether in the temple or on stage. Almost everything served to the divine couple is made of ghi (clarified butter), sugar, and spice, with flour or thickened milk and other ingredients to hold them together. The forms and varieties of such preparations are almost endless. In the līlās, when Rādhā and Krishna are eating together, each lovingly feeds the other choice morsels. Lover and beloved nourish each other not just with loving looks but with material food as well, and so all those who love the deity should both feed and be fed. The sakhīs run back and forth with baskets of sweets, while the svāmī describes the scene, and then one sakhī fetches a pitcher of water and pours it over the hands of Rādhā and Krishna into a metal bowl, and another brings a towel for them to wipe their hands. Another sakhī brings them betel leaf to finish their meal.

The svāmī sings poem after poem describing how they are enjoying their breakfast and the joy in their hearts. The sakhīs increase this joy by dancing and singing, and they bring in baskets of flowers to shower over the couple. This evokes the scenes in the *Bhāgavata Purāṇa* in which the gods, delighted with the child Krishna's feats, rain down showers of blossoms upon him. As the scene slowly unfolds, the songs emphasize that the love of Rādhā and Krishna is a special kind of love, a kind not to be talked about but just experienced. The beauty that radiates from the divine couple, he says, goes directly to the heart, and the image should be kept there by the devotee. This is darśana.

But soon an old monkey enters and announces that Rādhā and Krishna must leave immediately for their villages. The loving couple, in their confusion, put on each other's wrap—Rādhā takes the yellow silk cloth, Krishna the blue one. The sakhīs run off with the scattered ornaments and other things the couple has left behind, but Rādhā and Krishna linger a bit longer, unable to part. They embrace, very fondly but decorously. Krishna says that he cannot describe Rādhā's beauty; even if each hair on his body were a tongue, they would not be enough to tell of all her virtues. As the divine lovers slowly move offstage in separate directions, the svāmī continues to sing of their reluctance to leave one another and of their disheveled appearance and the scratches on their bodies after a night of lovemaking. He sings of the beauty of the divine couple, indescribable beauty too great for our eyes to see, too great for our tongues to utter. The couple, having slowly separated, rush together for a last embrace, and Krishna sings again of his great love for Rādhā:

My eyes are satisfied, my love, only when they see your eyes;
Numberless gods of passionate love I offer to your lotus face.
My mouth is happy only when it utters your pure name;
My hands are accomplished only when they adorn your lithe and graceful body;

My ears are pleased only when they hear your virtues sung;
My tongue can savor only when it tastes the nectar of your lips.
Fear does not vanish from my heart until I hold you in my arms;
My mind and heart, thought and interest are engaged only when I think of
your peerless form;
My peacock-feather crown has meaning only when I brush the dust from
your bed with it.
The sound of my flute is admired by the world only when it sings your virtues.
You are the ornament of my life—this vow I keep close to my heart.

Finally the curtain goes down. The svāmī sings that they have gone to their separate homes and gone to bed there. The houselights go up. It is six o'clock, and dawn has broken.

The Caitanya Līlā, First Day

Before the curtain goes up on the opening performance of the Caitanya aṣṭayāma līlā, the svāmī tells us that there is no difference between the līlās in Vraja and Navadvīpa, Caitanya's childhood home. As the curtain rises, we find Caitanya asleep in the garden of his disciple Śrivāsa in Navadvīpa, surrounded by five close associates. He is described as golden, surrounded by five gems—so beautiful that Kāma, the god of love, is envious. (Kāma is often said to be "defeated" by Rādhā's beauty.) The goddess of night enters and praises Caitanya, addressing him as Gaura (fair-complexioned, a name often used for him), as Krishna, as Rādhā, and as the divine couple. When she announces her departure, she calls in the mynah and the parrot, and together they sing of Caitanya's beauty and the pleasure of watching him sleep.

When Night departs, the goddess of the tulasī forest, Vṛndādevī, arrives, and she and the birds discuss the imminent awakening of Śacī, Caitanya's mother, and the fact that he should be in bed in her house when she awakes, or she will be distressed. Then the gods Śiva and Brahmā and the sage Nārada enter and join in singing the praises of Caitanya, and after a while they are joined by the great woman devotional poet, Mīrā Bāī. After more songs emphasizing that Caitanya is an incarnation of Krishna, the svāmī sings that whenever Caitanya remembers one of Krishna's līlās, that līlā takes place—and the audience sees, behind a netting curtain, a tableau of Rādhā and Krishna embracing.

When Caitanya finally awakens, he is described in terms reminiscent of descriptions of the divine couple. Then he washes and begins to perform his ecstatic chanting (*kīrtana*) as he goes to the Ganges to bathe. Finally, he reaches the door of his home, and his followers reluctantly obey him and leave him to go to their homes and sleep. Caitanya retires in his own bed, while servants massage his feet.

Second Day, 6:00 A.M.

The first performance in the Krishna aṣṭayāma līlā was a darśana of the nighttime tryst of Rādhā and Krishna, a glimpse of the awakening from the deepest mystery of the soul, but still in that magical world of the yogapīṭha. With the second līlā we awaken further, to the daylight world of Krishna, the son of Nanda and Yaśodā.

Before the curtain rises, we know something different is in store, for an area of the ground to the right of the stage has been fenced off. Just before the curtain goes up, four cows and a young calf are led into the pen and stand there placidly. At 6:00 A.M., just as the sky is growing light, Mahārāj jī again announces the beginning of this darśana, and the singing starts. The svāmī invokes the blessings of Yaśodā, Krishna's mother, who holds in her lap the boy Śrī Krishna, who is the foundation of the universe, and of Nanda, Krishna's father, who has carried on his back the cowherd boy who rules air, fire, and the moon.

After some time, two old women, their faces completely veiled by their red and yellow shawls, meet in front of the curtain. One is Yaśodā—she who believes Krishna to be her son. The other is the aged Pūrṇamāsī, traditionally identified as the old woman who knows all the women's rituals and instructs the younger ones. She has come to Yaśodā's house in the early morning to give her blessing. After inquiring about each other's health—these are grown men, speaking in falsetto—they go to wake Krishna.

The curtain rises, and we see Krishna asleep on his own bed, covered by a blue cloth that the audience recognizes as Rādhā's. The women try to waken him, calling him and saying that it is late, that the cows are waiting to be milked, and that he should join his father in the cowpen. But Krishna only buries himself under the blue cloth. Yaśodā, the doting mother, gossips with Pūrṇamāsī: he used to be a good boy, she says, and he went regularly with his friends and his older brother, Balarāma, to tend the cows. But the sakhīs have started teasing him—see the marks of their nails on his body, where they have scratched him—so he is unhappy about going out. Pūrṇamāsī says nothing; because the audience knows that later on she helps Rādhā and Krishna meet for a tryst, we suspect that she knows full well the source of those scratches and the reason for Krishna's exhaustion. Only Yaśodā seems totally immersed in mother-love for a son she sees as forever her darling child. "I am afraid for him," she says, "because he is a naughty boy and doesn't obey me. I am afraid he will be harmed by the wicked messengers of King Kaṁsa. Look," she says, "this mischievous child is wearing the blue cloth of his big brother, Balarāma" (the light-skinned Balarāma always wears blue; the dark-complexioned Krishna always wears yellow). Get up, Yaśodā says to the sleeping Krishna, the crickets are chirping, the women are churning the curd, and your friends are here to fetch you.

And, in fact, a troupe of cowherd boys dressed in yellow silk dhotis and shirts, with turbans of yellow, red, and pink, have come through the cowpen and are standing at the foot of the stage. They call to him, saying it is late, come milk the cows. Still, Krishna only turns over and hides under the blue cloth. The svāmī explains that Krishna cannot waken.

Now the sakhīs appear on stage, dressed in their bright silks of red, green, deep blue, vivid pink, and purple. In this context, they are no longer the handmaidens of the divine couple in eternal Vrindaban but—despite *our* ideas of how cowherd girls would dress—village women, gopīs, coming for darśana of Krishna. One says, "O Yaśodā, I touch your feet; I have come to see your son's face. Yesterday I saw his face as I was on the way to sell my curd and milk, and I sold it at a very good price. When I returned home, I found that my cow had given birth to a boy calf. After such good fortune, I want to see his face again, so that I may again have such good fortune." Yaśodā says she will arrange for her friend to have darśana.

Finally Krishna stirs and speaks—or, rather, recites a poem: "Please let me sleep. I am so tired, my feet ache, I can't wake up, and I certainly don't want anything to eat. After some time I will get up and go to the cowpen to milk the cows." But the boys insist, and they begin to dance and sing, making such a racket that Krishna stirs more actively. They finally rouse their sleepy friend, and Krishna gets up and embraces the boys as they dance and sing. Then he respectfully touches the feet of Pūrṇamāsi, and sits on the bed as Yaśodā performs *āratī*, circling him with an oil light on a tray that we can assume has the red powder, rice grains, and flower petals that are the standard offering of respect to the deity.

The seamless shift that is made in Yaśodā's behavior from innocent, doting mother of a naughty boy to the devoted worshiper of a divine child suggest that the two aspects are not separate, that any mother could see them both in her child at any time.

Now it is time to eat. Krishna is served by Yaśodā as he sits on his bed. The svāmī describes the bread and fresh butter, curd and dried fruits, nuts, apples, watermelon, and sweets that he is offered. After washing his hands, and after Yaśodā puts a flower garland on his neck and hands him the flute, Krishna leaves with his friends the cowherd boys.

As the svāmī describes the scene in poetry, Krishna and the boys go into the cowpen. The svāmī sings that although Krishṅa boasts that he is an expert at milking, he has to learn how to do it. The omniscient deity, in his human form, lets himself be taught all the skills someone in his position needs to know.

Meanwhile, Rādhā appears on stage, saying to herself that she must go see Krishna. Her mother asks her where she is going so early, and Rādhā replies that "yesterday you were angry because I was late, and the calves had drunk all the milk, so today I must go quickly so it doesn't happen again." In the Jaisingh Ghera līlā, the cowpen occupied the whole stage, and when Rādhā entered the cowpen, she and Krishna both milked cows that had been brought onstage—their eyes on each other the whole time. In Jaipur, Krishna was milking a cow in the cowpen at the foot of the stage while Rādhā stayed on stage, where she met Krishna's mother and, under her tutelage, began to churn some curd; at first, in her distracted state, Rādhā tried to churn an empty pot. All the time that this is going on, she and Krishna are gazing at one another, unable to concentrate. As Krishna milks the cow, milk spurts into the eyes of his friends; while he isn't looking, a calf comes to suck. All the while the svāmī is describing the scene, and those at the back of the audience who cannot see the action here at ground level in the cowpen (there are several thousand people, remember, all sitting on the ground) can see it in the mind's eye. Finally, the boys and Krishna depart in one direction, and Rādhā reluctantly joins the sakhīs to return to her house; she is overcome with the pain of separation from Krishna.

The next scene is a loving darśana of the bathing of Krishna and Balarāma. In the temple, the deity both bathes and eats in private, behind closed doors, so this is a very special darśana for the devotees. Krishna and Balarāma are seated on octagonal daises on either side of the stage, and although the poetry describes how Yaśodā bathes Krishna, on the stage Yaśodā stands to one side while Mahārāj jī, wrapped in his orange dhoti and shawl, performs the service.

From the devotees' point of view, it is wholly appropriate that Mahārāj jī be there. Just as in the temple the priest enters the deities' space to serve them, so in this context he does the same. Here Krishna plays not only in the eternal realm but also for all to see and hear and for Mahārāj jī to serve. Those in the audience can see at the same time the brahman boy from Vrindaban, whom many have known from childhood and watched fondly as he grew up and developed his talents as an actor—even as Yaśodā watches her son grow and learn—and simultaneously see him as a manifestation of divinity.

Krishna is not at all eager to be bathed. He complains that the water is cold, playfully jumps up and tries to escape, and then squirms under Mahārāj jī's firm grip. In preparation for the bath, his ornaments and garlands are removed, but his silk garments remain in place. Unguents are applied to his arms and legs, and then he is finally doused with pots of water. When, clean and chastened, he goes offstage to change, Balarāma is given the same treatment. As the good older brother, he resists less. The curtain goes down.

While the boys change into dry clothes, Yaśodā meets the sakhīs in front of the curtain and instructs them on what foods each of them is to prepare for breakfast—the earlier meal was just a snack. The svāmī describes for some time how happy everyone is to be serving Krishna and how their hearts are filled with love as they prepare the food. The curtain rises on Nanda's house, and we find Krishna and Balarāma seated on their daises on either side of the stage, with Mahārāj jī there to serve them. The svāmī sings that there are 170 kinds of food, calling to mind the breakfast served during the sevā in Rādhāramaṇa temple. The boys play as they are fed, teasing each other, their parents, and Mahārāj jī. The poetry lovingly describes in detail all the varieties of food they are eating, and the scene goes on for quite some time, ending with another āratī.

When the scene changes, we are in Rādhā's house, and she is behind a transparent pale blue curtain, surrounded by the sakhīs, preparing to take her bath. Again, Mahārāj jī comes on stage to help, but now his upper cloth is drawn over his head, like that of a traditional Indian woman, as he removes the ornaments and rubs on the unguents. Rādhā is not actually doused but wiped with water and again adorned with garlands and ornaments. Meanwhile, the svāmī sings of her beauty: "Love is showering from all parts of her body; she is the basis of all joy."

Then Rādhā, too, eats. She sits alone on one dais, while two sakhīs sit on the other one. The women are served a much simpler meal, followed by betel. When the final curtain comes down, it is 10:45 in the morning. So far we have had over seven hours of watching while, in fact, very little has "happened." And yet the audience feels that a lot has happened; they have been stirred by the rich visions and the music, while the poetry animated their imaginations and their memories of so many other times they had heard and seen these stories represented.

Although they are stiff and tired from sitting in the cold for hours, no one complains that it has gone on too long.

The Caitanya Līlā, Second Day

As we might expect, the second performance in the Caitanya līlā opens with the efforts of Caitanya's mother to awaken him. Then we meet the disciples on their way to Caitanya's house, who encounter two separate women in distress and offer them salvation through devotion to Caitanya. When they reach Caitanya's house, they play the role of the cowherd boys in rousing their leader, singing and dancing. Śacī is distressed by the dust and scratches on her son's body. (Though Caitanya has acquired the dust and scratches by rolling on the ground in his fits of ecstasy, the dust is like the dust that covers Krishna's body when he returns from the forest, and the scratches are like those inflicted on him during lovemaking.) It pains Śacī to see him so, she says, and she will not allow him to go out any more. She sounds very like Yaśodā, worrying about the young Krishna as he departs to tend the cows in the forest. "Do not speak like this," he replies, "because I cannot live without kīrtana [ecstatic chanting]. Just listening to kīrtana I start to dance, and sometimes I start to cry, and sometimes I lie down in the dust, and then I have no sense of what I am doing. . . . When I close my eyes, I see Krishna in my heart, and when I open my eyes I see Krishna in front of me, and when I go along the way, Krishna also comes with me, and when I see him behind me, I become faint and collapse. Krishna bores through my heart, I cannot live without Krishna."

When Śacī leaves to bathe in the Ganges, Caitanya is surrounded by his companions, who sing of his beauty and detail his attributes, much as the sakhīs sing of Krishna's charms. They declare that they cannot be separated from him. The svāmī sings that Caitanya is sitting in the courtyard, and bhāva (a feeling of devotion to Krishna) is coming into his heart. Such a feeling is not generalized, but quite particular: Vaiṣṇava theology has distinguished and analyzed the many bhāvas through which the devotee can cultivate a relationship with Krishna.[4] Some of the bhāvas are associated with particular activities (*līlās*); one of Caitanya's friends understands that the bhāva now coming over Caitanya is that of Krishna milking the cows, so he starts to sing the songs associated with the cow-milking līlā of Krishna, while Caitanya relives the scene. Caitanya then goes to take his bath in the Ganges, which he takes to be the Yamunā, chanting kīrtana ecstatically on the way; afterwards, he is dressed and ornamented by his associates. In the end, they are all served a large breakfast by Śacī.

Third Day, 8:24 A.M.

The two aspects of Krishna that dominated the first two līlās—Krishna the divine lover and Krishna the playful cowherd boy—come together in the third līlā, and the feeling (*bhāva*) of each context is explored more fully. Before the curtain opens, Mahārāj jī again reminds the audience that this is a worship of Krishna, that aṣṭayāma līlā is aṣṭayāma sevā (service). Everyone should therefore sit quietly and with attention, without saying a word.

The svāmī starts singing at 8:50 in the morning, and after a while the curtain opens on Krishna playing with the cowherd boys. As they dance and sing, the svāmī sings that Krishna is preparing to go out into the forest with the boys to graze the cows. Yaśodā is garlanding him and doing āratī. She is delighted by his beauty but worried that he may come to some harm: "Take care of your little brother," she says to Balarāma. "There are thorns and rocks on the path, and the sun is strong—let me give you sandals to wear," she says to Krishna. "It may rain, I shall give you an umbrella." Krishna replies that "the cows are my life. They wander in the woods without harm. The cowherd boys go barefoot, and when it rains they get wet. The cows and the boys manage in the winter cold and the summer's hot sun. I will take sandals and umbrella if you wish—but first you must give them to all the cows and cowherd boys. I am firm in this decision." The svāmī sings, "We must reverence the god who treasures cows and brahmans." (Reverencing brahmans as well as cows tends to come into verses of the *Bhāgavata Purāṇa*, as in this poetry, whenever acts of benevolence and piety are described; an outsider cannot help but think this a self-serving sentiment on the part of the authors, but the devotees do not hear it this way.) So the boys set off for the forest with their cows, represented now by two boys on hands and knees, in white suits and cow-head masks. They all go down the steps that now descend from the stage to the audience's level, and the boys sing and dance in the space in front of the audience.

The forest of Vrindaban has a very special place in Vaiṣṇava imagery. It is an idyllic place of green grass, flowering trees, and running water. For those who live in the present town of Vrindaban, this description is particularly poignant, for it depicts what is painfully missing amid the crowding, decay, and pollution of the town. It is what the pilgrims are invited to picture as they trudge along the lanes or walk barefoot on the path that forms a ring around Vrindaban.

The forest is, above all, not the city. It is where the heart and mind are free to feel the beauty that is their natural food. This forest is sometimes invaded by demons, but Krishna playfully defeats them. It is the place where the strict rules that control the ordinary lives of people in India do not exist. Krishna and his companions play and tease the girls and women, who complain but love him dearly and are completely charmed by his beauty. These stories of Krishna's sports, which are the subject of the popular imagery of Vaiṣṇavism—in stories, paintings, and the rāsalīlās—are the basis of the aṣṭayāma līlā, but depicting them is not the chief intention of this dramatic form. The aṣṭayāma līlā is rather an extended exploration of Vrindaban as "the forest of the heart"—the space and time of the inner world, the world of the soul. When Rādhā and Krishna are with their families and friends, they are still subject to the obligations of the world—although it is an adoring world, apparently entirely at their service. In the forest, they are free and, in their natural condition are beautiful without limit and joyful as long as they are together. The aṣṭayāma līlā, like sevā in the temple, is a prolonged meditation on the real nature of the soul—bliss, ānanda.

As the boys proceed to the forest, the svāmī describes the clothes and ornaments of this divine cowherd boy (Figure 19). He wears a peacock feather on his head and a flower garland on his neck. Silver bells are tied around his ankles. He wears a cowherd boy's short pants, says the poetry (on stage he wears a yellow silk dhoti or tunic), and a yellow upper cloth, tied with a silver girdle. His bracelets are made of jewels set in a net of gold, as are his armbands. There is an ornament in his nose (instead, on stage, patterns are painted on cheeks and forehead), and he wears gems on his fingers. His ear ornaments hang and swing against his cheeks. Balarāma is wearing blue, Krishna is wearing yellow; Balarāma plays a horn, Krishna his flute. The cows, hearing them, prick up their ears and tails and, filled with love, trot faster along the path—so says the poet.

The cowherd boys follow Krishna joyfully, each carrying a stick with a bundle on the end, which soon enough they will untie to reveal a picnic snack. After a while the troupe mounts the steps to the stage, and the curtain opens to reveal a forest scene: trees hung with flowers are in the background. The cows are set to grazing. The svāmī sings that "we are the servants of the cows. Cows are our mother, father, and guru. Cows are our god, we are always aware of them. . . . They give us everything we ask for. . . . The whole countryside is a field of cows." (Vraja, the region around Vrindaban, literally means "cowpen" or "place where cows roam.")

The boys begin to play. The *Bhāgavata Purāṇa* lovingly describes their games:

Figure 19. Krishna (front) and Balarāma.Vrindaban, 1992.
Photo by Robyn Beeche.

Thousands of Śrī Krishna's dear cowherd boys came out of their homes and joined him, carrying slingshots and walking sticks, horns and flutes, and driving their thousands of calves before them. Their own calves mingled with the innumerable calves of Śrī Krishna, and they began to wander from place to place, playing childhood games. Although every boy was decorated with beads and seeds, gems and gold, still they decked themselves with the red, yellow, and green flowers of Vrindaban, with tender new leaves, bunches of multicolored flowers, and peacock feathers, as well as dabs of red clay and other colored minerals.

Some of them stole one another's slingshots, others stole walking

> sticks or flutes. When the owners of these things found them, then the ones who had taken them flung them further away, and a second time threw them still further. Then, laughing, they returned them. . . . Some boys played on flutes, some blew horns. Still others hummed with the bees, and called "kuhū, kuhū" with the voice of the cuckoo birds. In one direction, some cowherd boys were chasing the shadows of birds that flew in the sky; in another direction, some were walking gracefully alongside some swans, imitating their movements. Some were sitting with herons, closing their eyes like them; some, watching peacocks dance, were dancing like them. Several of them, grabbing the tails of monkeys, were pulling them . . . several were making faces at the monkeys, and others were leaping from branch to branch with them.
>
> Many of the cowherd boys were playing, splashing along the banks of the river, and were leaping about with the frogs who hopped there. Some of them, seeing their reflections in the water, laughed at them, and others shouted abuse at the echoes of their own words.
>
> Bhagavān Śrī Krishna is known by experienced saints to be himself the conceptual image of Brahmā's delight. For devotees tied to him by the feeling of service, he is the deity whom they wish to serve and worship with abundance. For those who are charmed by the pleasures of māyā, he is only a human child. With this very Bhagavān, those fortunate cowherd boys played in this way. (X.12.2-18)

On stage, there is darśana of the boys playing. Balarāma leads the way by starting to dance, and soon all the boys are dancing in a circle, weaving in and out in patterns of a folk dance. A pair of peacocks appears—boys on their knees, supporting with their arms a fan of feathers that rises over their heads behind them. All the boys imitate the birds, and Krishna does the peacock dance, whirling on his knees, though without the peacock feathers that he usually wears when doing the peacock dance in the rāsalīlās, which the devotees eagerly expect and applaud.

Next the boys wrestle with one another. One then imitates the musicians, who are sitting on the left side of the stage, and another mimics Mahārāj jī, who stands on the right side waving a cow-tail fan. Then they play various ball games until they are tired. All the while, the svāmī sings, describing the games. Finally, he sings of the meaning of all this: "The happiness of the people of Vraja is greater than the happiness which people in heaven can even dream of. For they have the supreme god as a friend. The world says he is Indestructible, but in every home in Vraja he is a playmate."

Now a couple of birds—boys in cloaks and bird masks—come onstage and describe Krishna's beauty, with the svāmī supplying the words from the apparently inexhaustible ocean of poetry on this theme. The audience is again bathed with the images and associated feelings of love and devotion.

Soon the boys complain of being hungry after all their playing, and they open their bundles. They play around for a long time as they eat the food. Mahārāj jī serves them water to drink, and when some is spilled, he wipes up the puddles with a cloth. Finished eating, the boys lie down to rest. When they are all asleep, Krishna sneaks off for a tryst with his beloved.

As he goes on his way, in front of the curtain, Krishna sings praises of Rādhā. Meanwhile, Rādhā decides to test his love and dresses up as a cowherd boy. The next scene is the most prolonged piece of theater—as distinguished from tableaux vivants—so far.

Krishna, on his way to meet Rādhā, encounters this unknown boy on his road. "He is so beautiful, he is very dear to me. I will go ask him where he is from, and become his friend." The disguised Rādhā says, "My name is Priyatam [sweetie], and people call me Piyāro; eight cowherd boys are my friends." "Really?" says Krishna, "I also have eight cowherd boys as friends! So we are a good pair. We will be friends from now on."

But Rādhā hesitates. "I have always been doubtful about you, and a little afraid of you, and this is why I have never come near here to graze my cows. I just forgot, today, and that is why I came, and now see what happened!"

"Why should you be afraid of me, and what happened to you today?"

"Today I lost my calf, and I heard he might have gone to your cowpen. Do you have my calf in your cowpen?

"No," says Krishna, "I don't—who told you this?"

"When I went with my cows to search for him, when we went to your village, the cowherds were sitting on a platform, and I greeted them and asked them about my calf, and they told me that in our Vraja there is a thief, Nanda's son. Go and look in his cowpen, they said, so I came here."

Krishna, taking the accusation in stride, asks, "How can you recognize your calf?"

"He is beautiful, white with reddish marks on his back, and his tail has a lot of hairs, like a fan. His eyes are black with eye lining—he is the most beautiful calf we have. So tell me where he is, if you please."

"I don't think your calf is with me, but we can go see if he came with the other cows. If you don't find your calf, you can choose three or four beautiful calves from among mine, and take them."

But Rādhā says, "By your grace, we already have many calves, but that one is very beloved. Since he is not in your place, shall I go? I will see you somewhere else."

But Krishna stops her: "Just listen—one thing, I want to make you my friend, so please be my friend."

"Friendship is proper only when the two are equal; what kind of friendship can we have when you have big cows and I have little ones?"

"That will make no difference to our friendship. We will always stay together."

"If you insist, we will be friends—will you take *kuā* [well] or *kiyārī* [flower bed, in which shallow water is retained]?" This is a child's saying, contrasting depth with breadth of feeling, which cements a friendship.

Krishna says, "Kiyārī—then you and I are friends."

When they have agreed to be friends, Rādhā asks with a smile, "Tell me truly, which cowherd's daughter is your beloved?"

Krishna says, "She is more beautiful than the beloved of the god of love, more beautiful than Lakṣmī herself; Rādhā is my beloved."

But the disguised Rādhā says, "Oh, you have made a great mistake, she is not good enough for you, your love is wasted on her."

"However much I praise her virtues, even if it is embarrassing to speak about her so much, I cannot live without talking about her—and I tell you because you are my friend."

But Rādhā says, "You don't know her very well, that's why you love her."

"I know her well, and I cannot hide from you what kind of girl she is. She always walks with her eight friends, carrying a pot of curd on her head, and as she wanders through the forest she sells her curd with pride—so she is not an ordinary girl. People say she is a king's daughter, but she doesn't put on airs like one."

Rādhā tries another tack: "I know another girl for you—she shines more brightly than many goddesses, gods of love, and moons put together. She is very clever in all the arts of loving. Like a waxing moon, the beauty of her body is quickly increasing. You would be good for her and she is suitable for you—she is more beautiful than anyone in all three worlds. Once I talked about you in her house, and her mother became very happy. She asked me everything about your family and where you live, and so on. I didn't tell them about any fault you might have, only the good things, and she wants an engagement with you. She said: 'My daughter is very ready for this match, and I will give her.' If you think that I'm not telling the truth, then see this letter that they gave me, and read it for yourself. You should marry that girl immediately. You should get married in the spring—don't delay. And no matter where you search, you will never find a girl like this."

Krishna says nothing, but he is very angry.

Rādhā continues: "Only when you see her will you believe how beautiful she is. She is so beautiful that Lalitā and all the sakhīs will seem like her servants to you. If I'm wrong, we can just forget it, but you should think about it. You will be happy when she comes to your house; you will be really impressed with her beauty."

Krishna finally explodes: "Just get up and go home—get out of here! You are insulting Rādhā, and it makes me very angry."

Rādhā says, "I thought I was telling you good things. I only wish you well."

"What you say does not please me, they are very bad. I controlled my anger for a long time, because your complexion is very fair, like Rādhā's, but these words are hostile, not the words of a friend. I can no longer tolerate them, though your face and color look like those of my beloved. The beautiful girl you told me about—I did not like that. I only like people who admire Rādhā in front of me, not those who admire other girls. . . . In so many ways there is no comparison with Rādhā. Rādhā's virtues are so profound, you cannot touch bottom. . . . You are coarse, you could not recognize Rādhā, you cannot understand her value, how precious she is. A tradesman selling hot peppers and salt cannot evaluate a diamond; only a jeweler can recognize its value. Rādhā is a sacred pool, and I am a swan on its surface. Rādhā is an ocean of beauty, and my heart is a fish. I say Rādhā when I stand, and I say Rādhā when I sit. When I wander I say Rādhā, and I speak her name with my flute. I am always singing Rādhā's virtues, and I live to speak her name. Without seeing her, I cannot drink water. Saying Rādhā, Rādhā, I take the cows for grazing, and saying Rādhā I come home . . . and saying Rādhā, Rādhā, I become Rādhā. Rādhā is my body and I am Rādhā's body. So, my dear friend, listen, we have one heart and two bodies. . . . How can you understand this mystery, that we are not different?"

By now the audience is in tears, feeling Krishna's distress.

"Why are you wasting your time saying Rādhā all the time? I will only believe you if you call your dearest Rādhā here right now."

"I can't call her just now, don't insist."

"I will only believe you really love her and she loves you if you call her here right now."

"All right, if you don't believe me, I will just call her. You stay here." Krishna closes his eyes and begins to pray with folded hands, saying, "Please help me, Rādhā." Putting his flute to his lips, singing her virtues, remembering her at every moment, he prays for her grace. "When I was in trouble, you have always helped me, Rādhā. Help me now. When

Indra deluged Vraja with rain, and I lifted Mount Govardhana, you helped me, how else could I have done it? You took all the weight of that mountain on your eyebrows, just by looking at me. However much I say about your virtues, Rādhā, however many virtues you have, I have that many failings, so now listen to me and relieve me of this trouble. If you and I are not different, then come immediately."

While his eyes are closed, Rādhā goes to the wings, and Krishna continues to praise her, begging her to come. Rādhā suddenly appears in her own clothes and asks, "Why do you keep calling me?" He opens his eyes and is overcome with joy. They embrace, and immediately the sakhīs appear and garland them, make them sit, and serve them food. For many minutes, they sit and lovingly feed one another choice morsels. Then, after they have washed their hands and had some betel, the sakhīs do another āratī and the curtain falls. It is afternoon.

The Caitanya Līlā, Third Day

The Caitanya līlā for this period of the day also plays with the testing of the protagonist's love, in ways that bring into play human dilemmas that are only hinted at in the Krishna līlās. Tradition says that Caitanya left his wife and mother to take vows of renunciation. That he should leave them to fend for themselves was heart wrenching. A sannyāsī is traditionally dead to his family; he can have no further contact with them. In the līlā, before Caitanya leaves, both women plead with him not to go; when he does depart, their sorrow echos that of the cowherd women when Krishna leaves them, but it also mirrors the gopīs' own separation from their families to be with Krishna.

The opening scene of the Caitanya līlā depicts the two women pleading with him to stay. Soon, however, someone mentions the name of Krishna, and Caitanya loses consciousness and in his mind lives the scene of Krishna and Balarāma going with their friends to the forest with the cows. As Caitanya wanders around the garden, lost in the world of Vraja, his companions sing of his beauty; then the great god Brahmā and the sage Nārada enter and sing his praises. Their theme is that, in today's world, hearing and reciting the name of Krishna (through chanting—kīrtana—and the recitation of "Haré Krishna") is the best way to invoke his presence. Brahmā, the Creator, says that Caitanya is "the incarnation of love and sympathy in the Kali yuga. I don't want the position of Brahmā, although I am the founder and father of this world. I need to rest in his lotus feet."

In the next scene we find an old woman, anticipating her death and insisting that the name of Krishna be whispered in her ear as she dies, for the name of the Lord will save her. For the rest of the līlā we have interweavings of this theme, with scenes of Caitanya and his friends enacting the games of Krishna and the cowherds in the forest. The denouement is a scene of all the friends as they eat together.

EIGHT

SEEING KRISHNA

Aṣṭayāma Līlā Continued

So far the līlās have followed a day in the life of Krishna fairly literally. Now time and space open up, as it were, and the annual cycles of the ritual calendar are enfolded within the enactment of the daily cycle.

Fourth Day, 10:48 A.M.

Midmorning is when the first playful energies of the cowherd boys are spent, and one might imagine it to be the time when their leader, the boy Krishna, leads them on many of his famous escapades and adventures. But although these pastimes of Krishna are sometimes elaborated upon in the rāsalīlās, the aṣṭayāma līlā concentrates on the eternal relationship between Krishna and Rādhā, and in this time, at the midpoint of the cycle, we are transported into another dimension—the ritual cycle of the entire year. In the aṣṭayāma līlā staged in Jaisingh Ghera in 1992, the "fourth day" was, in fact, split into two, and all the major festivals of the year were observed: *candana yātrā*, when Krishna is adorned with sandalwood paste; *jala yātrā*, when fountains play in the temple during the hot season; *jhūlana,* the swing festival of the monsoon season; the fall season and the great circle dance; the winter with its cold; and finally Holī, the great spring festival. As though to emphasize that the time and space of the aṣṭayāma līlā is not the same as worldly time, an entire year was compressed into this midday time slot in the twenty-four hours of Krishna's life. There were elaborate special effects for these līlās—fountains, thunder and lightning, showers, swings, and a carriage pulled by bullocks-in-costume.

In Jaipur, only two līlās were played in this midday performance: the stealing of Krishna's flute by the cowherd girls—one of the most frequently enacted episodes in the troupe's repertoire—and the celebration of Holī.

The theft of Krishna's silver flute is a story with a simple plot.[1] The flute is his inseparable companion, whose notes summon all creatures to his company and whose melody conveys all the sweetness of Krishna's being. It is stolen by the cowherd girls, who are jealous of Krishna's attachment to it and irritated that whenever he plays it they are compelled to drop their work and follow its summons. The girls revel in possessing it; Krishna bemoans its loss, pleads with the girls to return it, accepts Rādhā's arbitration, and admits to her that he is lost without it; although she says justice does not demand its return, she hands it back out of compassion. This episode is often the first one to be presented in a cycle of rāsalīlās, and so to present it here is to open up the entire cycle, to draw in to the aṣṭayāma all the well-known stories of Krishna's mischievous and charming youth.

Although the distinction is one of degree alone, the presentation of the theft of the flute in the aṣṭayāma līlā differs slightly from that in the standard rāsalīlās in that there is less horseplay and more expression of the feelings of love and loss through the poetry. The theme is familiar, the story well known, and what is cultivated is the exquisite play on the images and themes to arouse bhāva in players and audience alike.

This is again true in the presentation of the celebration of Holī. Holī is the last date of the Rādhāramaṇa ritual calendar and thus marks the end of one ritual year and the beginning of another. The rāsalīlā of Holī is also the final one in the cycle presented in Jaisingh Ghera in the spring; in this sense, to present it here finishes the entire cycle in this one performance.

At Holī, people celebrate the coming of the new year. The villages of Vraja hold their celebrations on various days over a two-week period on either side of the full moon of Phālguna, and each village has different customs associated with the festival. Two elements are very widespread: throwing colored powders or water, and setting a blazing bonfire under the full moon. The mood of everyone is festive, and some people travel from village to village to enjoy the celebrations in each. It is a time of joy and also of license. Everyone knows the boundaries are loosened, that anyone can do anything to anyone else—in theory at least—though in polite society the boundaries in general hold firm, the only breach being license to throw colors on all and everyone.

In Vrindaban, pink and green powder is thrown on passersby in the streets for three days before the climactic day of the full moon. In Rādhāramaṇa temple, the evening āratīs are preceded by an hour of samāja (group singing) led by Mahārāj jī, while the priests on the platform throw colored powder and squirt colored water on those who come for darśana. On the night of the full moon, a great bonfire is lit at various temples, including one outside the compound of Rādhāramaṇa temple. On the next morning, the day of the "saturnalia," the color throwing gets rougher, as boys and young men play Holī in the no-holds-barred spirit that prevails in the villages.[2] For a few hours, it is not safe for women to go out in the street. By midday, it is all over, and people start cleaning up themselves and everything else that has been colored pink, green, red, yellow, and purple.

Inside Jaisingh Ghera, there is a safe haven until the morning of the saturnalia. Early in the morning of the day before, eight hundred pounds of flowers are prepared: their petals are removed and piled in baskets, to be thrown as the climax of the līlā to be played on stage. Everyone sits around in groups on the floor of the great hall, joining in this pleasant task. In the rāsalīlā, which begins about 10:00, the sakhīs and the cowherd boys tease and taunt each other for a while, and then all the boys in the troupe join in showering Rādhā and Krishna, who are sitting on a throne, with basket after basket of the flower petals, burying them in the yellow, white, and rose. There are fountains and showers of flowers on stage, and then the petals are thrown at the audience. As the līlā ends, the audience scoops up handfuls of the petals and flings them at each other.

On the morning of the saturnalia, which is also Caitanya's birthday, there is a samāja (group singing) in Jaisingh Ghera, which takes various forms from year to year, but which is generally led by Mahārāj jī or his son Veṇu Gopāla. After this, those who want to play Holī with colors gather with their syringes and colored water in the courtyard to douse each other and any unwary passerby, and anyone else who can be coaxed to join the fray. The boys, some of the servants, and foreigners are usually the most enthusiastic participants, though often Mahārāj jī and his sons join in for at least a while. Traditionally and ideally the color has been brewed from yellow flower petals; this color is mixed with arrowroot powder or with water. In recent years, aniline textile dyes have also made their appearance. Because of this, those who have fair skin and light hair tend to be pink for weeks afterward.

In Jaipur, Holī as it was played in the aṣṭayāma līlā was a time of color, beauty, love, and joy, without the taunting and teasing that occur as a prelude in the rāsalīlās of Holī. When the curtain rose on this part of the performance, Rādhā and the sakhīs were in the forest, where flowers hung from all the trees, not singly but in bunches. The women had baskets in their arms and were wandering here and there, picking the flowers for playing Holī. Rādhā and Krishna, each with a dish of colored powder, chased each other playfully and gently, and lovingly put colors on each other's faces. Meanwhile, the sakhīs threw handfuls of color on the white coverings of the stage wings. The atmosphere was joyful, while the svāmī sang traditional Holī songs. Then Rādhā and Krishna sat on their throne and were buried in flower petals by the sakhīs. When all the flowers had been piled on them—Mahārāj jī came over from the sidelines twice to brush the piles off their heads so they could breathe—they got up, and the sakhīs made a big pile of the petals on the stage. They all gathered around, and scooping up the petals in their arms and tossing them up in the air, they made a golden fountain of flowers. Again, they gathered them in a pile, but left a space in the center, and Rādhā and Krishna whirled around, holding hands, while the sakhīs doused them with the golden shower. Thus a familiar theme was elaborated, like a raga, to create the wished-for emotion of joy in players and audience.

The Caitanya Līlā, Fourth Day

When the curtain opens on the fourth episode of the Caitanya līlā, Caitanya is sitting in Śrīvāsa's garden—a garden famous as being the place where he practiced the ecstatic kīrtanas that became his characteristic mode of worship. The garden is described in terms that evoke the forests of Vrindaban, and the associates who are gathered around him address him with devotion and adoration, saying they are filled with emotion and want nothing more than to touch his lotus feet. Enters a "baby" gathering flowers to worship Krishna; she says her name is Dukhī, "sorrowful"; Caitanya says that no one in this place can have such a name, and renames her Sukhī, "happy," and she exits joyfully. The men also leave, singing and dancing.

In the next scene, Caitanya's wife, Viṣṇupriyā, enters, saying that she is sorrowful because she never sees her husband, and she cries that without him her life is nothing—a theme familiar from the lament of the cowherd women when Krishna leaves them. Again, we shift to Caitanya and his friends, who are singing:

> We see his beauty in every part of his body. How can I express this? It can only be experienced. Caitanya is dancing, his long arms raised, and

> with him all the people of Nadiya village are dancing with so much pleasure. . . . O is it Caitanya or is it Śrī Krishna? He is dancing with holy music for the welfare of mankind. Caitanya is dancing with love and affection for Śrī Krishna. Sometimes he falls unconscious on the earth from emotion, lying stretched out in the dust, becoming senseless—and all the members of the devotees' group became sorrowful.

Soon food is served, all described in detail by the svāmī. Then Caitanya goes to the bank of the Ganges, and soon falls into ecstasy, believing that it is the Yamunā and he is Krishna, whose flute has been stolen. Then he wanders into a beautiful garden, whose flowers are described in the poetry, and he evokes the coming of spring and the throwing of the colors at Holī. Soon all the associates are singing and dancing, playing at Holī. In the next scene, it is the rainy season, and Caitanya and all his companions sing the appropriate songs; at the end, Caitanya swoons in ecstasy.

Fifth Day, 3:36 P.M.

Up to this point, although the action of the aṣṭayāma līlā had spilled over into the space in front of the stage, it was confined to the front of the hall or tent. Preparations on the fifth day in Jaipur in 1995 made it clear that the area of action would be expanded (though the script was very similar to that of the fifth day in Vrindaban in 1992). A wide lane was created down the center of the tent, between the men's and women's sections. Ropes running from back to front were stretched on either side of the lane, supported on flower-covered stanchions and wrapped in gold ribbon. A white cloth was laid in the pathway, and yellow-orange flower petals were thickly strewn over it. To the side of the area in front of the stage, where the cowpen had once stood, there was now a tall lookout tower, decorated in blue ribbon and gold. On the other side of the stage, a balcony was constructed and hung with yellow-orange garlands.

As the curtain opens, we see the cowherd boys asleep under the trees, taking their afternoon nap. Krishna sneaks in, returning from a rendezvous with Rādhā, and quietly lies down among them. Soon Balarāma stirs, stretches, and realizes that it is late. He calls the other boys, and they all wake up, except Krishna, who is now sound asleep. But they shake him, and soon he, too, gets up, and all the boys sing and dance together; one boy sings that they all belong to Vraja—and he includes the audience with the sweep of his hand—and because of this there is no barrier of caste among them. The boys' songs are now in praise of Mount Govardhana. The annual celebration of Govardhana pūjā in the fall, when the mountain is honored on the day after Dīpāvalī (Dīwālī, the festival of lights in honor of Lakṣmī), includes the preparation of enormous quantities of food to offer to the deity—the mountain itself, which is the body of Krishna—or to Krishna in any temple; the "leftovers" are shared as prasāda by the devotees, sometimes as a neighborhood feast in the temple courtyard. Here, in the aṣṭayāma līlā, no food is immediately forthcoming. Instead, the boys begin again to play games—varieties of drop the flag and line tag. Soon enough, they become hungry and quickly eat the food they have brought with them. Mahārāj jī, ever present with his cow-tail fan on the sidelines, pours water for them.

Still complaining of hunger, the boys next go to the forest to pick fruit. They find bananas, apples, and papayas hanging from the trees. Krishna climbs a tree—onto a platform hidden among the branches—and throws fruit down to the boys and to Mahārāj jī, who catches a large papaya thrown to him. Having eaten the fruit, the boys are still hungry, and there is some playing around as they steal a basket of food one of the boys has been hiding.

But now the boys are still complaining of hunger. One, who is lame, says he feels as if two pigeons are fighting in his stomach, he is so hungry, and after some discussion the boys decide to steal some beans growing in a nearby field. They start to do that but are chased away by a watchman and narrowly escape a beating. They decide to go, instead, to some bean fields in Barsānā, Rādhā's village. When they arrive there, they stealthily enter the fields and start to eat the beans. A watchwoman sees them and they all run, but she catches the lame boy and starts to beat him. The other boys, standing on the side, laugh, and finally she lets him go. As all the boys run away, Krishna drops his yellow silk scarf. The watchwoman picks it up, complaining that the boys have ruined her field, and declares that she will complain to the king of Barsānā, Rādhā's father, Vṛṣabhānu.

The next scene takes place in the king's home, and the watchwoman complains to the royal couple. They reassure her and keep the yellow scarf, which they recognize as Krishna's. Seeing it, love wells up in their hearts—the same kind of love as they feel when Rādhā is sitting with them. It is said in the *Bhāgavata Purāṇa* that Krishna has the extraordinary quality that all people love him as if he were their own son. Her parents call Rādhā, saying that if she wears the cloth, their joy in seeing them both together will be doubled. The parental love with which they are filled—described by the svāmī—is a counterpoint to another love felt by Rādhā, whose body thrills at the touch and smell of Krishna's cloth. Her mother and father send her out to play, and she resolves to find Krishna.

The scene shifts back to the boys, still playing.their games when they realize that it is late, time to find the cows and take them home. Krishna calls the cows with his flute and then calls them by name. Mooing (there is a moo-cow squawk box offstage), they come, represented by four boys on hands and knees, in cow costume.

By now, the sun has set and the hall is dark. A spotlight picks out three deities standing on a platform at the rear of the pavilion, surrounded by the audience: Śiva, Brahmā, and the sage Nārada, often understood to be an incarnation of Viṣṇu.[3] They proclaim their devotion to Krishna in Vrindaban. The effect is to include the whole audience in the time and space of the līlā. They are not just all people of Vraja, they are part of this eternal līlā.

Next the spotlight illuminates Rādhā in her tower on one side of the stage and several girls in their balcony on the other side, all waiting and watching for Krishna and the boys to appear. The svāmī sings the poetry of their anticipation. Soon we see the boys and cows at the back of the flower-strewn pathway.

"Cow-dust time" is a very special time in the Indian aesthetic—the time when the cows return home along the dusty paths, and the slanting sunlight of evening turns everything golden. The *Bhāgavata Purāṇa* (X.21.2–5) describes it as the time when the village women begin to think of Krishna's return to the village, and begin to look for him. The poets also, taking up this theme, have left a rich body of poetry, and the svāmī sings some of these poems for forty-five minutes while the boys very slowly move up the path. This is a very special darśana, for the audience is put in the position of villagers gathered at the side of the road, watching Krishna and the boys who follow the cows home (Figure 20).

While they are advancing, Mahārāj jī places clay lanterns with small oil lamps along the front of the stage as a welcome to them. Finally, the boys reach the front, mount the steps, and are greeted by Yaśodā, who does the early-evening āratī for them, just as it is done in the temple.

The Caitanya Līlā, Fifth Day

The fifth installment of the Caitanya līlā starts earlier in the day, at 1:30, so when Caitanya returns home along a path lined with townspeople

Figure 20. Krishna and Balarāma bringing the cows home. Jaipur, November 1995. Photo by Robyn Beeche.

who watch his progress, it is for lunch. Along the way a singer chants of his love for Caitanya, called by his nickname, Gaura. It is a song often included by Mahārāj jī in his gatherings:

When I sleep I see Gaura, in my dreams, there is Gaura;
My wealth is Gaura, my life is Gaura, my death is Gaura.
Gaura is the garland of my neck—tell the stories of Gaura continually.
Gaura's name is like ambrosia—it gives pure love.
If I say Gaura and then die, what else do I need?
Gaura is devotion, Gaura is salvation, Gaura is the essence of the Veda.
When he walks, his body makes me smile;
When he speaks, his words seem like nectar in my ears;
The word Gaura is a treasure, and lifts my heart.

The singer of this song in the līlā is a cobbler, who is now abused by the brahmans, and he complains that they always treat him like that because he is of low caste. The svāmī sings:

> It doesn't matter what caste you come from, if you feel love for Krishna, you can meet with God, and you can sing in his praise. Whoever is proud of his high caste, he is a fool.

But still the cobbler complains that, as he is low caste, he cannot achieve the love of Krishna:

> When will I go to that Vrindaban of love? When will I get rid of my worldly ties? When will my eyes be lined with the eye-black of knowledge? When will all parts of my body be covered with dust? When will I become a renunciant forever? When will I take water from the Yamunā of love with both my hands and drink it? And when will I be mad with love, when will I drown in the ocean of happiness? And become mad myself, and make everyone mad? And take shelter in the lotus feet of Krishna?

When Caitanya enters, he embraces the cobbler, as he also does a cowherd who comes along, saying no one will associate with him because he is untouchable. And then Caitanya and his companions continue on their way home, singing kīrtana and proclaiming that this is the way to know Krishna. The message is not that social ranking must be done away with but that social ranking is irrelevant in pursuit of knowledge of Krishna.

The gods Brahmā and Nārada enter and comment on the procession. In the Kali yuga, the present age, they say, singing kīrtana is the only means of worship: "In Satya yuga [the golden age]," says Brahmā, "people follow the path of knowledge; in the next age they sacrifice; in the third age, they do sevā; but not in Kali yuga—I see they do not do these forms of worshipful practice, they do only kīrtana." "Yes," replies Nārada, "and the results are the same in each age; by doing kīrtana in this age you get even more results." And so they resolve to follow Caitanya as he proceeds home, to be welcomed—and fed—by his mother.

Sixth Day, 6:00 P.M.

The sixth performance is scheduled to start at 6:00 P.M., and in Jaipur the pavilion has returned to normal, except for a small cowpen just below the stage on the right, where, as the performance begins, four boys in cow costumes perch on a platform. But there is some special excitement among those in charge of arrangements for the performance. Soon enough, the Mahārāja of Banaras arrives and is seated on a rug in the front of the audience, next to the eldest son of the chief priest of Govindadeva temple (Figure 21). The Mahārāja is well known for his patronage of Rāmalīlās (plays based on the life of Rāma) in Varanasi, and he has long sought and received guidance from Mahārāj jī.[4]

As the curtain goes up, Krishna and Balarāma are offered buttermilk by their mothers. Then, while the svāmī sings of the boys' beauty, the mothers remove their sons' ornaments in preparation for washing the dust off their arms and legs. Although the poetry says that Yaśodā washes Krishna, again onstage it is Mahārāj jī who does so. This finished, the boys go off to milk the cows. In front of the curtain, on his way to the cowpen, Krishna meets three cowherd girls in succession. Each of the first two asks him to come milk her cow, for he is a great milkman and the cows give more milk to him. It is clear that Krishna has also stolen

Figure 21. The Mahārāja of Banaras, November 1995. Photo by Robyn Beeche.

their hearts. The third girl is more overcome by the encounter. Krishna embraces her, and she loses consciousness.

The mood changes as the cowherd boys come in, and they all go to the small cow pen. The svāmī sings that they are all milking the cows.

Now it is again time to eat. The curtain rises on Nanda sitting at home, with Krishna and Balarāma on either side, eating. The svāmī describes all the things Yaśodā is offering to them and prays, in the words of the poet, that he might receive some of the leftovers as prasāda. Then there is an entr'acte. Krishna sits in a tower (brought in to stand on the platform where the "cows" had perched), and Rādhā is in the balcony to the left of the stage. The two gaze at one another while the svāmī sings of their happiness and wish to meet each other.

Now the *sāñjhī līlā*—another celebration with firm roots in Vrindaban practice—is played. For several days in the late summer, unmarried village girls create sāñjhī patterns—designs and pictures—of clay, flowers, and bits of pottery on the walls of their homes and then perform their devotions in front of them in the evening, in hopes of getting a good husband. In some Vaiṣṇava temples, the priests spend all day laying out intricate patterns of colored chalk on octagonal clay platforms on the floor of the temple to depict scenes from Krishna's sports and deeds. The devotees come to admire them in the evening.[5]

On stage, Rādhā and the sakhīs stand in front of the curtain, holding decorated baskets, and say that, since the day of sāñjhī has come, they will go pick flowers in the forest. They go off, and the curtain rises on a forest scene, with flowers everywhere in the trees. There is a well on the left side of the stage, and Krishna is drawing water and putting it on the trees while singing of his pleasure in being in the forest. He lovingly names all the flowers and mentions the humming bees, mad with the fragrance of flowers; he names all the birds that are singing and describes the peacocks dancing; he says that a cool breeze is blowing. Vrindaban, he says, is an ocean of joy, but without his dearest, Rādhā, he cannot really enjoy it. "Sāñjhī is a gathering of joys, but my life is my dearest Rādhā, and without her I cannot be happy. Your face is the lotus, my eyes are the bee . . . your curly locks are my shelter, and taking refuge in them my heart becomes confused. . . . I will be straight and clear again only when I see your simple, pure face. . . . You will come here to pick flowers for sāñjhī, and I am sitting here, hoping to see you." As the girls approach, he hides among the trees.

Now there is a disjunction in time and space. As Rādhā is wandering among the trees and bushes, a garment she is wearing is caught on a thorn. Unable to free herself, she calls the sakhīs—but it is Krishna who appears. This līlā is usually taken as a representation of the first meeting of Rādhā and Krishna, for now apparently in a fit of forgetfulness, she doesn't know who he is. Their eyes meet and they stand transfixed. The svāmī sings, "When your garment is caught by a thorn, you can remove it. But when your eyes are caught by another's, who can remove them? Then Krishna freed Rādhā's garment from the thorn, and the two hearts ached for each other." Not just their hearts were affected, says the poet:

> The ocean of joy is increasing in the body of Krishna. Looking at the full-moon face of Rādhā, the high tide of the heart rises in Vrindaban. On one side the Yamunā forms a barrier, on the other side the cowherd women try to limit it, but something—bliss—just spreads in the three worlds. Sage and yogi, they are unable to attain this, but it is fixed in the heart of the those who can enjoy the scene. Gradually, by the power of their wisdom, they are bathing in this rasa. The līlās change at every moment for the devotees. . . .

So it does not matter that this līlā of a "first encounter" should occur near the end of the cycle of performances. The development of the bhāva is very high, the expression of love between Rādhā and Krishna is without guile or complication, and those who have witnessed the earlier darśanas are prepared now for this one.

Slowly the couple part, and Rādhā rejoins the sakhīs, telling them of her encounter. "I don't know his name, but his complexion is dark, and his scarf is yellow. Take me there again to pluck flowers in that forest."

They all go off, and soon they come to the wood where Krishna is tending the trees. Krishna challenges them: "What are you ladies doing here, without someone watching over you? You should be concerned about your safety, and your reputation. You should go home instead of wandering here—or else you should explain to me why you are here." When the sakhīs disrespectfully begin to call him names, Krishna claims guardianship of the forest, including the right to exclude others.

A sakhī replies, "What is 'others'? All things are Rādhā's. This earth is Rādhā's and all birds and deer are Rādhā's. All morning and evening, they say only Rādhā, Rādhā. All the ponds, all the trees are Rādhā's; all the flowers and fruits are Rādhā's; this Vrindaban is Rādhā's, and is proclaimed as Rādhā's. So why are you blocking our way?"

Krishna capitulates: "I am also Rādhā's, please accept me. Only by seeing her moonlike face do I stay alive. Call me near, and give me shelter—you all are very dear friends of Rādhā, so don't think badly of me. Now you have defeated me, everything here is yours. But please give me some respect, because I am taking care of this garden. Otherwise, you can take whatever you wish."

The sakhīs indulge in more banter, but the svāmī sings, "Krishna stands in front of Rādhā with folded hands, he is gathering confidence in front of her, but he cannot tolerate her limitless beauty, for she looks like the blue sky with the moon. His eyes are like the *chakora* bird's, watching that moon; his legs are trembling, his yellow silk garment is falling from his hand. Seeing her, he has no steadiness; sinking in the beauty of her form, he cannot speak or act. He wants to take control of his heart, but it is out of control."

As the sakhīs sing of their love, Rādhā puts a garland around Krishna's neck, bringing to mind the beginning of the Hindu marriage ceremony, when the bride and groom garland each other; for most of the wedding guests, this is the climactic moment of the hours-long ceremony. Then Rādhā and Krishna embrace and turn to admire the sāñjhī decorations that have been on two octagonal platforms—one in dried fruits and nuts, befitting the winter season in which the līlā is actually being played, the other a floral pattern of red, yellow, and white petals.

The līlā comes to an end with Rādhā and Krishna once again seated at a table while the sakhīs serves them food.

The Caitanya Līlā, Sixth Day

The sixth performance of the Caitanya līlā has even less of a story line than the others. It is filled with songs of Caitanya's beauty, of the need to worship him and the need to sing kīrtanas. Caitanya's friends are with him as he bathes in the Ganges, as he sees Krishna playing the flute, and as he goes with them for supper at his mother's house. It is a virtually unalloyed development of the themes of devotion and love of Caitanya.

Seventh Day, 8:30 P.M.

The seventh līlā, starting at about 8:30 in the evening, began with some after-dinner entertainment for Krishna's father, Nanda, the king of the cowherds. He sat on a throne with his two sons, under the red-cloth columns. The entertainment was different in the two productions of 1992 and 1995, depending on the availability of talent. An important feature in 1992 was a dance by Sonal Mansingh, before whom the black bee had first appeared. In Jaipur, the first entertainers to come in were a troupe of the men, devotees of Mahārāj jī, who had been in charge of all the local arrangements. Dressed as Vaiṣṇava kīrtana singers, they sang a long song in praise of Krishna. Then two of the "cowherd boys" who had acrobatic skills performed, as did the musicians who had accompanied the singing throughout the līlās. Finally, the boys were summoned home by their mothers, who welcomed them with milk in golden bowls, and after drinking it the boys went to retire.

But retiring from the daytime family world does not end the day for Krishna and Rādhā, and each of them goes to the forest at night to search for the other. In 1992, the theme of *virāha*—longing in separation, a very widely developed theme in devotional poetry—was developed for a long time. This is the *mādhurya līlā,* the līlā of sweetness, which is a līlā of sweet pain that moves people as none other does. Rādhā and Krishna begin by playing a game of hide-and-seek, but soon they really cannot find each other. As each wanders in the forest, searching for the other, the audience is moved to tears by the sorrowful words of the svāmī.

The aṣṭayāma līlā in Jaipur included some of the same poetry, without the story line. First we see Rādhā wandering in the dark forest, while clouds gather and thunder rumbles. The svāmī sings:

She is going in the dark night, very slowly, stepping carefully.
The forest trees all want to see this scene.
Preparing herself carefully, well, she is going to meet the moon of Vraja.
Who is going? She who also has a face like a moon. . . . .
The whole garden is filled with lotus blossoms, wherever Rādhā puts her feet. . . .
Diamonds on the edge of her black sari and pearls falling from her hair look so lovely.

The images and similes not only evoke the many times and contexts in which they are used in poetry but also bring to mind the many paintings that have been done on this theme. Because it is presented in the spirit and context of awakening people's feelings, it does not seem jaded, but fresh and moving.

And again the svāmī sings, as Rādhā wanders, searching desperately from tree to tree:

The wind blows her sari and the creepers are blowing in the wind.
The water of the river moves in circles.
The night is very dark, the river is making a loud noise, and the clouds are rumbling as they move in the sky.
Thunder roars and lighting flashes continuously, not stopping for a moment.
Rādhā wants to meet with Krishna, and she goes to the bower,
Sometimes filled with desire, sometimes halting with fear and then going on.

As she goes offstage, Krishna enters, distractedly looking for Rādhā. Finally, they meet as the storm breaks. Embracing, they take shelter in the forest. The reunion of lovers in the monsoon is another favorite theme of poets and painters, and innumerable miniatures come to mind as the words are sung:

The two of them are getting wet, when they come to the bower;
As the raindrops hit them, their love grows stronger.
When the clouds make more noise, they hide under a tree.
Krisha puts his yellow silk cloth around Rādhā, and Rādhā puts her cloth around him.
Seeing this beauty, the cuckoo sings;
In the midst of the clouds, the wind blows, and Krishna plays the rain raga on his flute.
Both the lovers are getting wet, and their wet bodies look very beautiful.
In this way, says the poet Surdāsa, divine love grows.

Rādhā and Krishna find a swing in the bower; first Rādhā swings, and then Krishna, while the svāmī sings of their loveliness. They swing together, and then the sakhīs come to them and lovingly serve them food and betel. The audience, which has stayed despite the late hour—it is now about midnight—and the cold, feels nourished by the darśana.

The Caitanya Līlā, Seventh Day

The seventh performance of the Caitanya līlā develops the theme of Viṣṇupriyā's pain of separation from her husband. The couple sit together, singing of their love for each other, but then Caitanya leaves, and Viṣṇupriyā again complains of being abandoned. "I offered everything in your feet, became a *yoginī,* why are you leaving me? I cannot understand; I am only alive when I am with you, so don't leave me alone." It is a theme that evokes the women's sorrow when Krishna left them, but its tone can also appeal to the feelings of every woman in the audience who feels neglected by her husband.

When Caitanya leaves, he goes to the riverbank and hears Krishna's flute. Now he loses consciousness and is lost in Vrindaban, where the mādhurya līlā is being played. Rādhā and Krishna enjoy each other's love in the forest bower, served by the sakhīs. They play hide-and-seek, are separated, and finally are reunited to swing together in a forest grove as the rainy season starts.

The Eighth Day, 10:00 P.M.

In Jaipur, people begin to sit in the pavilion early, as they come for the last darśana of Govindadeva jī in the temple at 8:30, and stay on.[6] As performance time approaches, the pavilion becomes full, despite the hour. There are three segments to the final līlā. First, the curtain opens on Rādhā and Krishna embracing and enjoying the beautiful forest. Then she decides once again to test Krishna and sulks, refusing to let him near her. He pines and goes off in great distress. On the way, he meets the chief sakhī, Lalitā, who promises to plead his cause with Rādhā. On her first try she in unable to change Rādhā's mind. Then Lalitā and Krishna scheme, and we see Lalitā telling Rādhā that there is a wonderful exhibition of pictures she should see. Rādhā wants to see it, and they go. When the curtain opens on the exhibition, various pictures of deities are hung on a wall, and in the middle stands Krishna, framed, with a thin net curtain in front of him. He stands in his triple-bent posture, fluting. Rādhā looks at the pictures, and when she comes to Krishna, she is quite enchanted and wants to have the picture. Lalitā says she can get it for her, and Krishna steps out of the frame. Happily, they embrace.[7]

The next scene is the *mahārāsa līlā*, the great circle dance, considered the culmination of the Vrindaban līlās of Krishna. The curtain opens on Rādhā and Krishna with the eight sakhīs, in the forest. Krishna is no longer wearing yellow but has on a multicolored dancing skirt. Everyone moves into a circle, dancing in slow steps and making various dance patterns. Then they move faster, and Krishna whirls on his knees—the peacock dance. The scene captures the flavor, the essence of the mahārāsa, without the story, which involves multiple Krishnas dancing with the sakhīs, disappearing, and being found again.

When they are all tired from the dancing, Rādhā and Krishna sit on a throne and are served food. Smiling, they lovingly serve each other, drink from golden vessels, and are served betel. Āratī is offered to them, and at last they retire in the bower in the shape of a lotus blossom in which we first found them eight days—twenty-four hours—previously. The bower is now surrounded by gilded and silver foliage. As Rādhā lies on the platform, Krishna massages her legs. A net curtain is drawn in front, as Mahārāj jī fans them with his cow-tail fan. As they both lie down, the curtain falls. It is one in the morning, and the time until they awaken before dawn is not to be viewed by human eyes. The crowd departs through the dark and silent streets.

The Caitanya Līlā, Eighth Day

Before the curtain opens on the final līlā of the Caitanya aṣṭayāma līlā, the svāmī sings that the son of Śacī sings and dances on the courtyard of the house of Śrīvāsa under the full moon, chanting the divine names, with tears running down his cheeks and his hair standing on end, encircled by his devotees, until he retires to his bejeweled bed. This is the plot summary of the performance, but there are interruptions to the chanting, each of which tells a story that illustrates one of Caitanya's qualities.

First, as Caitanya and his companions are chanting, Caitanya suddenly says, "Where is that flute I hear?" The scene swiftly changes to Vrindaban, where one sakhī asks another, "Where is that flute I hear?" Krishna is standing there, calling Rādhā with his flute, and they dance together, pausing after every few moves in an intertwined position, suggesting their inseparability—as they are inseparable in Caitanya (Figure 22). After dancing, they enjoy the beauty of the forest, and then a small dispute—called the "pique līlā"—erupts; finally, Krishna submits to Rādhā, and they sing together again.

The scene changes back to Navadvīpa, where the group is chanting and dancing with Caitanya. Abruptly Caitanya stops the kīrtana, saying, "Śrīvāsa, I am not enjoying kīrtana because there is a hypocrite, with external consciousness, among us." Śrīvāsa replies that an ascetic whose only food is milk asked to be allowed to see the kīrtana, "so I took him as someone devoted to your feet and allowed him to come in." Caitanya is furious, saying, "Do you think drinking only milk will bring devotion? Fish drink only water, snakes drink only air, goats eat only grass, rats live under the earth, the lion lives in the deep forest—do they get devotion to the Lord? Various heroes underwent incredible perils, but did they get devotion? An untouchable is more dear to me than a hypocritical ascetic."

The ascetic throws himself at Caitanya's feet and says, "I am very grateful to you for relieving me of my burden of the arrogance of penance." Seeing his devotion, Caitanya embraces him, and the kīrtana returns to its former tempo.

As they are dancing, the most senior devotee, Advaitācārya, stoops to take the dust from under the feet of Caitanya and blesses himself. After a few moments, Caitanya stops and says, "Today the kīrtana does not reach its usual tempo. Have I made a mistake, or has someone touched my feet without my knowing it?" Wishing to avoid arrogance, he did not allow others to touch his feet in respect. When he learns that it was

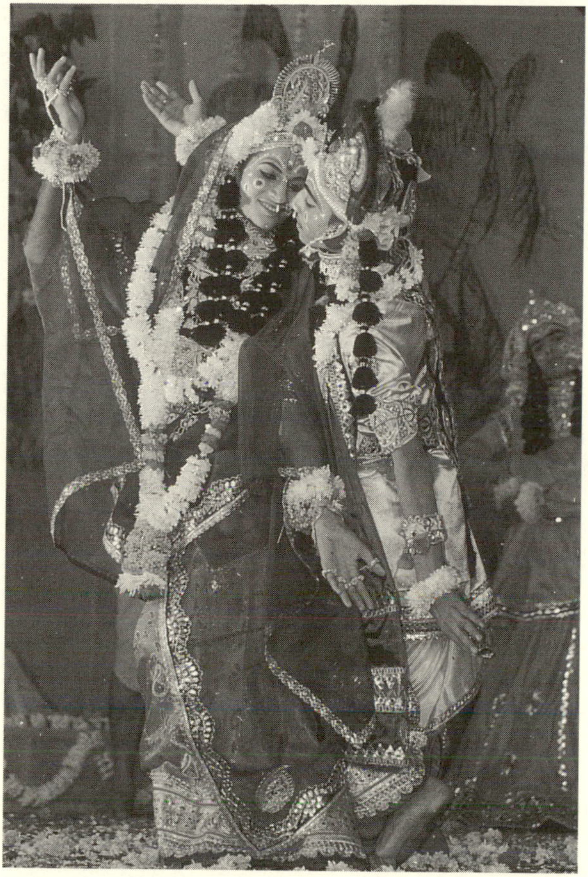

Figure 22. Rādhā and Krishna intertwined, as one person. Jaipur, November 1995. Photo by Robyn Beeche.

Advaitācārya who had, in effect, touched his feet, he makes the old man lie on the ground, and then Caitanya rubs his own head against the soles of his disciple's feet. The other devotees follow suit, and Caitanya laughs and says that Advaitācārya is receiving his punishment.

Next comes a somewhat more complicated depiction of Caitanya's social message. The kīrtana reaches a crescendo, and Caitanya falls unconscious on the ground. Intoxicated by devotion, his disciple Murārī goes home to his house to take his dinner, but as he tries to eat, his food keeps dropping to the ground. As the women repeatedly fill his plate, and the food keeps dropping, Murārī says over and over, "You eat, you eat." Finally he eats a bit himself, the women do kīrtana, and he falls asleep. In the middle of the night, Caitanya comes to his house and says, "I am having terrible stomach pains, why did you feed me so much? I must drink water to lessen the acidity." Caitanya thereupon picks up Murārī's water pot and drinks from it. Murārī is horrified, for the water pot has been polluted by his own mouth, and tells Caitanya that for that sin he will go to hell. "No," says Caitanya, "today I drank nectar from the lips of my own devotee."

In the final scene, Caitanya is talking with Śrīvāsa, asking him how he provides for his family since he does no work. Śrīvāsa says, essentially, "The Lord will provide. If I go three days without food, my body will go in the river." Caitanya, impressed, promises him that he will never be poor, and at this everyone falls at his feet. Finally everyone eats, and Caitanya falls asleep, surrounded by his companions.

EPILOGUE

This book began with the appearance of the black bee, which was accepted by Mahārāj jī and his devotees as a manifestation of Krishna. I said that I was often asked whether I believed that this was, in fact, Krishna. My answer: within the context, yes—and context is everything. The quest to see divinity and the question of whether what was seen *was* divinity can be addressed only within context. The seer is a seeker, not passive, but with an active role to play. What is seen, though profoundly personal, is not idiosyncratic but understood by a community to be a manifestation of divinity. And the experience is supported by a narrative—by stories that are traditional, living in memory, and re-created at each telling or enactment.

Vrindaban is redolent with narratives of saints who have seen Krishna there, beginning with the cowherds and their families and continuing through a sometimes vague historical time to the present. Most visions are strictly private and immaterial, but they include the solid, stone appearance of Śrī Rādhāramaṇa in the sixteenth century. For him and other images discovered at the time of Caitanya Mahāprabhu, the original great temples of Vrindaban were built. These embodiments of Krishna continued to be served in the temples by the families—spiritual and biological—that controlled them. The brahmans who conduct the services around the clock claim as a fact, without a trace of irony, that they know Krishna. Ordinary people and the pilgrims who witness the public portions of their service can share in some small part of this knowledge through darśana, seeing. This, too, is accepted as a fact.

But one need not be a priest within the inner sanctum to participate in Krishna's activities. Serious devotees visualize and are privately aware of Krishna's activities throughout the day. More visibly, both those who serve Krishna by acting in the rāsalīlās and those who witness the līlās come from a large pool of Vaiṣṇavas who are in every stage and condition of spiritual development. In the last two decades, Mahārāj jī has further broadened the opportunity for darśana by conflating performance and service both inside and outside the temple. The priests' round-the-clock service to Krishna in the temple has been transmuted into the less ritually stringent, more playful, but equally worshipful aṣṭayāma līlā, and the special effects from theater performances have been brought into the temple during Mahārāj jī's period of sevā. Within the context of the ritual or performance—temple service or aṣṭayāma līlā—Krishna appears, and the perception is that there is no difference between the sacred image in the temple and the child playing Krishna in the aṣṭayāma līlā. Involvement—participation of brahmans and lay devotees both inside and outside the temple—thus validates new boundaries for the appearance of divinity. And in the perception of the Goswamis and devotees alike, the intense rituals carried out at Bhramara ghat opened the way for the appearance of Krishna in the context of a narrative that was related to that specific place.

The place, the time, and the stories were crucial. I hope that what I have described demonstrate that. What I have not conveyed are the brackets on either side as it were, of this experience: the normal, daily life of this world on the one side and the transcendental life encoded in esoteric knowledge on the other.

Daily life in Vrindaban, as in the rest of India, leaves little of the human condition to the imagination. Filth, stench, wretched poverty, illness, cruelty, arrogance, and indifference coexist with sublime craftsmanship, devoted service, gentleness, and kindness. The climate runs to extremes; public services, including electricity, are erratic; good intentions constantly run afoul of pressing demands and urgent distractions. But one very rarely sees people express frustration or anger: the roads are hazardous, for example, but "road rage" is not one of the dangers. In the West, we are used to laughing at small accidents, mishaps, or others' discomfort; in Vrindaban, the threshold between laughter and concern is much higher, and more is accepted as part of the unexpected, laughable aspect of life. This, to me, is the bracket on one side of the pervasive devotional life of Vrindaban. This is what faith brings to daily difficulties—a kind of joy as well as acceptance of what, after all, often cannot be changed.

On the other side, the meaning of the texts and rituals is not exhausted by the rich correspondences between story and enactment that enliven the celebrations and dramatic productions of Vrindaban. There is much deeper knowledge within Vaiṣṇava tradition that can be approached by specialists in the knowledge of the divine, the initiated priests. Very few, to be sure, have the desire or capacity to pursue that knowledge, but it remains as a living tradition among a few teachers, available to those who are qualified. Without that knowledge behind it, the power of the tradition would be lost.

The Goswamis hold that it is possible for any individual to bridge the space between the two brackets by participating as fully as possible in Krishna's līlās. As initiated priests in the Rādhāramaṇa Gosvāmī lineage, they not only participate as individuals but also provide various venues for the līlās to be played. Mahārāj jī, as impresario, facilitates the līlās that lie at the heart of seeing Krishna. He creates a context within which darśana is possible. But the seeing—and the believing—are up to each person.

NOTES

Prologue

1. A. K. Ramanujan has discussed the context-oriented basis of Indian culture in "Is There an Indian Way of Thinking? An Informal Essay," in *India through Hindu Categories,* edited by McKim Marriott (New Delhi: Sage Publications, 1990), pp. 41–58.

Chapter 1

1. An abbreviated version of this chapter was published as "The Birth of a Shrine" by Shrivatsa Goswami and Margaret Case in *Parabola: The Magazine of Myth and Tradition* 18.2 (May 1993): 31–36.

2. Translations from the *Bhāgavata Purāṇa* are my own, from *Śrīmad Bhāgavata Mahāpurāṇa* (Gorakhpur: Gītapres, n.d.), in Hindi.

3. See John Stratton Hawley, *Krishna, The Butter Thief* (Princeton: Princeton University Press, 1983) for an extensive discussion. The disciplining of young children, especially boys, in India today seems imbued with the same loving indulgence showed by Yaśodā to Krishna.

4. See Barbara Stoler Miller, *Love Song of the Dark Lord: Jayadeva's Gītagovinda* (New York: Oxford University Press, 1977); Kenneth E. Bryant, *Poems to the Child-God: Structures and Strategies in the Poetry of Sūrdās* (Berkeley and Los Angeles: University of California Press, 1978); and John Stratton Hawley, *Sūr Dās: Poet, Singer, Saint* (Seattle: University of Washington Press, 1984).

5. See David Haberman, *Journey through the Twelve Forests* (New York: Oxford University Press, 1994), for a description of the various sites.

6. See David L. Haberman, *Acting as a Way of Salvation: A Study of Rāgānugā Bhakti Sādhana* (New York: Oxford University Press, 1988).

7. See Irfan Habib, "A Documentary History of the Gosā'ins (Gosvāmīs) of the Caitanya Sect at Vṛndāvana," in *Govindadeva: A Dialogue in Stone,* edited by Margaret H. Case (New Delhi: Indira Gandhi National Centre for the Arts, 1996), p. 156, citing a document dated 1704: in the mid-sixteenth century, "the village of Bindrāban [Vṛndāvana] . . . was full of jungle and uninhabited."

8. See Haberman, *Journey through the Twelve Forests*, pp. 32–33; and Alan Entwistle, *Braj: Centre of Krishna Pilgrimage* (Groningen: Egbert Forsten, 1987), pp. 275–76.

9. An extraordinary glimpse of the lives of these devotees may be had in Habib's "A Documentary History," in which he translates texts that document grants to the temple and disputes over land and grants that were settled in the courts of various rulers in the seventeenth and eighteenth centuries.

10. They included the philosopher Baladeva Vidyābhūṣaṇa, Paṇḍita Kṛṣṇadeva Āgamavāgīśa, the architect Vidyādhara (who designed Jaipur), and a galaxy of scholars of astrology and astronomy. The information in this and the next several paragraphs was given me by Shrivatsa Goswami.

11. The shrine was moved in 1962 to make room for construction of a rāsalīlā hall, and after three and a half decades the image was given a new permanent shrine, dedicated on Hanumān's birthday in 1996.

12. This sixteenth-century text by Kṛṣṇadāsa Kavirāja is being translated by Neal Delmonico. Selections of that translation, with an illuminating introduction, may be found in *Religions of India in Practice,* edited by Donald S. Lopez Jr. (Princeton: Princeton University Press, 1995), pp. 244–62.

13. *Bhedābheda,* difference in non-difference, is a fundamental tenet of much of Hindu philosophy and postulates the integration rather than the duality of opposites. Acintyabhedābheda is a concept formulated by Caitanya's follower Jīva Gosvāmī to express the relationship of Krishna's powers (*śakti*s), embodied in the sakhīs who attend him and Rādhā, to his own true form or essence (*svarūpa*): inconceivable difference in non-difference. The term is more loosely applied by the Goswamis to other instances of nonduality.

14. This style of reading is done in such a way that a full reading of the text is completed in a week. One-seventh is read each day; the traditional stopping points are III.21, V.14, VII.15, X.2, X.54, XI.13, and XII.13. The year after this was begun, the Yamunā River, which except in monsoon season had for many years retreated to a shallow bed on the other side of the flood plain, returned to the shore of Vrindaban outside Jaisingh Ghera. The Goswamis believe that this was in response to the readings; it reinforces their belief in the spiritual basis of environmental protection.

Chapter 2

1. Most of the information on Mahārāj jī's life was supplied by his son, Shrivatsa Goswami, in conversation and in his paper, "The Role of the Guru in the Caitanyaite Tradition," presented at a conference on the "Role of the Guru" in Ahmedabad in January 1997. The rest of the information comes from

conversations with Mahārāj jī himself, with other family members, and with devotees.

2. Nita Kumar explores wrestling as an integral part of the north Indian ideal male lifestyle in *The Artisans of Banaras: Popular Culture and Identity, 1880–1986* (Princeton: Princeton University Press, 1988), especially chapter 5. "Mahārāj jī" is a common honorific among religious leaders, just as the title Rāja is loosely bestowed on the major landowner in a town.

3. *Bhāgavata Purāṇa,* "Śrīmad Bhāgavata Māhātmya," vv. 61–62.

4. Readers familiar with this material will notice that I use the term "Caitanyaite" rather than "Gauḍīya," the more common term for the sect (*sampradaya*). I follow here the argument of Shrivatsa Goswami, who argues that although Caitanya was a Gauḍīya—that is, he came from Gauḍa in the southwestern part of Bengal—he established Vrindaban as the headquarters of his movement, and he himself spent most of his life in Orissa. "Gauḍīya" is thus a misnomer. See, for this argument, his paper, "The Role of the Guru in the Caitanyaite Tradition."

5. John Stratton Hawley, in association with Shrivatsa Goswami, discusses the rāsalīlās of a troupe sponsored by Mahārāj jī in *At Play with Krishna: Pilgrimage Dramas from Brindavan* (Princeton: Princeton University Press, 1981).

6. David Haberman, *Journey through the Twelve Forests* (New York: Oxford University Press, 1994) is an account of one such vana yātrā and of the history, stories, and practices connected with it.

7. O. B. L. Kapoor, *The Saints of Vraja* (Caracas, Venezuela: Śrī Caitanya Bhakti Rakṣaka Maṇḍapa, 1992), an English translation and abridgment of his two-volume compendium on the subject, gives the stories of many of these holy men. On darśana, see Diana L. Eck, *Darśan: Seeing the Divine Image in India* (Chambersburg, Pa.: Anima Books, 1981).

8. The girl's brother told me this story; a close devotee of Mahārāj jī told me a version in which a young girl who drowned when Mahārāj jī was on pilgrimage to Haridwar was brought back to life by him. This is an example of how legends grow, even among those closest to the principal figure.

9. On the Tantric elements in Vaiṣṇavism, see Edward C. Dimock Jr., *The Place of the Hidden Moon* (Chicago: University of Chicago Press, 1966).

10. I am especially grateful to Shrivatsa Goswami for elucidating this relationship in conversation.

11. The translations of the sādhānikā are mine, with the assistance of Shrivatsa Goswami, from his Hindi translations printed in the booklets. The previous verses are from the *Bhāgavata Purāṇa* II.9.30–36.

12. T. R.V. Murti expressed this fundamental philosophy very succinctly in *Studies in Indian Thought: The Collected Papers of T.R. V. Murti,* edited by Harold Coward (Delhi: Motilal Banarsidass, 1983), pp. 335–36.

13. This hymn is described by the scholar Prabhat Mukherjee as "dubiously ascribed to Chaitanya" in *History of the Chaitanya Faith in Orissa* (Delhi: Manohar, 1979), p. 52 n.19.

Chapter 3

1. As Edward Dimock, the dean of American scholars of Vaiṣṇavism, explains, "Food, like everything else, consists of *gunas*, the qualities which give an object its distinctness. Physical *gunas* give rise to form, distinguishing one object from another. And coterminous with these *gunas* is a set of nonphysical ones that lend an object its essence. It is essence, not form, that is intrinsic, nourishing, and pleasing to God." Edward C. Dimock, "Bhakti," in *Cooking for the Gods: The Art of Home Ritual in Bengal,* edited by Pika Ghosh (Newark, N.J.: Newark Museum, 1995), p. 30.

2. I was present at the place where she stayed in Mumbai from a few minutes after her death until leaving on a train that evening; I did not arrive in Vrindaban until after the cremation but heard several accounts and saw detailed photographs taken by Michael Duffy. I was present throughout the mourning period in Jaisingh Ghera.

Chapter 4

1. Although I have drawn on various experiences, conversations, and readings in my understanding of Caitanya, this chapter leans even more heavily than other portions of the book on the interpretations of Shrivatsa Goswami.

2. There are four world eras, or yugas, in a day in the life of the creator god, Brahmā. The fourth and most degenerate, the Kali yuga, in which we live, began, according to Vaiṣṇava belief, with the death of Krishna.

3. A brief, sober biography of Caitanya in English may be found in Prabhat Mukherjee, *History of the Chaitanya Faith in Orissa* (Delhi: Manohar, 1979). Edward C. Dimock Jr. wrote an interesting analysis of the problems in Caitanya's biography in "On Impersonality and Religious Biography: The 'Nectar of the Acts of Caitanya'" in *The Sound of Silent Guns and Other Essays* (Delhi: Oxford University Press, 1989), pp.102–12. See also the Ph.D. dissertation by Tony K. Stewart, "The Biographical Images of Kṛṣṇa-Caitanya: A Study in the Perception of Divinity" (University of Chicago, 1985).

4. Mukherjee, *History of the Chaitanya Faith*, pp. 19–20.

5. Karen Pechilis Prentiss, exploring the interpretation of bhakti as "participation" rather than "devotion," has examined the south Indian tradition in her book, *The Embodiment of Bhakti* (New York: Oxford University Press, 1999). I am grateful to her for letting me see her manuscript before publication.

6. Mukherjee, *History of the Chaitanya Faith*, pp. 21–37.

7. On the choice of the Six Gosvāmīs and the settling of Vrindaban, see Shrivatsa Goswami, "Govinda Darśana: Lotus in Stone," in *Govindadeva: A Dialogue in Stone,* edited by Margaret H. Case (New Delhi: Indira Gandhi National Centre for the Arts, 1996), pp. 270–71.

8. Mukherjee, *History of the Chaitanya Faith,* p. 41.

9. The primary source on which almost all others draw is the *Caitanyacaritāmṛta* ("The Nectar of the Acts of Caitanya") of Kṛṣṇadāsa Kavirāja. A translation by Edward C. Dimock and Tony Stewart is due to be published at some future date

in the Harvard Oriental Series. A short hagiographic biography in English is *Lord Gauranga* by Shishir Kumar Ghose ([1961] Bombay: Bharatiya Vidya Bhavan, 1990), a condensed English version of his two-volume work by the same name; there is also an 800-page Bengali version, *Śrī Gaurāṅga.*

10. *Bhāgavata Purāṇa* X.45.36.

11. Ibid., X.23 and 24.

12. Ghose, *Lord Gauranga,* p. 52.

13. See Shrivatsa Goswami, "Rādhā: The Play and Perfection of *Rasa*" in *The Divine Consort: Rādhā and the Goddesses of India,* edited by John Stratton Hawley and Donna Marie Wulff (Berkeley: Berkeley Religious Studies Series, 1982), pp. 72–88.

14. See Harold Coward, ed., *Studies in Indian Thought: The Collected Papers of T. R. V. Murti* (Delhi: Motilal Banarsidass, 1983), p. 337.

15. This paragraph and the next few summarize conversations with Shrivatsa Goswami, especially one on November 6, 1996.

Chapter 5

1. Much of the material in this chapter has appeared in my article, "Sevā at Rādhāramaṇa Temple, Vṛndāvana," *Journal of Vaiṣṇava Studies* 3.3 (Summer 1995): 43–57.

2. See R. Nath, "Śrī Govindadeva's Itinerary from Vṛndāvana to Jayapura, c. 1534–1727," in *Govindadeva: A Dialogue in Stone*, edited by Margaret H. Case (Delhi: Indira Gandhi National Centre for the Arts, 1996), p. 161.

3. A. W. Entwistle, *Braj: Centre of Krishna Pilgrimage* (Groningen, Egbert Forsten, 1987), p. 147.

4. Ibid., pp. 155–56.

5. It is interesting that the closely related Rādhāvallabha temple is also served by separate sublineages, in this case only two. See ibid., p. 179.

6. Rādhāramaṇa temple (called Rādhārawan) received a land grant from the Mughal emperor Akbar in 1598 C.E., according to Tarapada Mukherji and Irfan Habib, "Akbar and the Temples of Mathura and Its Environs," *Proceedings of the Indian History Congress* 48 (1987): 234–50.

7. F. S. Growse, *Mathurá: A District Memoir,* 3d ed. (Allahabad: North-Western Provinces and Oudh Government Press, 1883), pp. 262–63.

8. This is the "founding story" also told by the Goswamis. A different version is told by Entwistle, *Braj,* p. 219. According to him, the present Rādhāramaṇa temple was built in 1826 by a Seth from eastern India named Bihārīlāla, who was given the title Shah by the nawab of Lucknow. One of his grandsons, who had settled in Vrindaban and taken the name Lalitkiśorī, built Shahji Mandir in 1868 in the Italianate style then fashionable in Lucknow. Entwistle's source is A. L. Kapur, *Vraj ke bhakti* (Mathura: Śrī Kṛṣṇa Janmasthān Sevāsaṃsthān, 1980–1982), vol. 3, pp. 1–12.

9. The whole flowering of Hindu spirituality explores and develops this theme of the logic of the relationship between human and divine. One helpful

discussion, using the materials of another branch of Hinduism, is Richard H. Davis, *Ritual in an Oscillating Universe: Worshiping Śiva in Medieval India* (Princeton: Princeton University Press, 1991).

10. Robyn Beeche was present for these events and reported them to me.

11. I am grateful to Advaitacaraṇa Gosvāmī for this information.

12. For a discussion of the various styles of temple music, see Guy L. Beck, "Havelī Saṅgīt: Music in the Vallabha Tradition," *Journal of Vaiṣṇava Studies* 1.4 (Summer 1993): 77–86; and his "Vaiṣṇava Music in the Braj Region of North India," *Journal of Vaiṣṇava Studies* 4.2 (Spring 1996): 115–47.

13. The original images of both Gokulānanda and Rādhāvinoda, for whom the temple was established, went to Jaipur in the eighteenth century, but full service of the substitute images is maintained here.

14. See Shrivatsa Goswami and Robyn Beeche, *Celebrating Krishna: The Living Theatre of Vraja,* in preparation.

Chapter 6

1. See the various articles in *Govindadeva: A Dialogue in Stone,* edited by Margaret H. Case (New Delhi: Indira Gandhi National Centre for the Arts, 1996). This heavily illustrated volume collects papers given at a conference on Govindadeva at Jaisingh Ghera in April 1991.

2. The information in this section is drawn from Gopal Narayan Bahura, "Śrī Govinda Gāthā: Service Rendered to Govinda by the Rulers of Āmera and Jayapura," ibid., pp. 195–213, and R. Nath, "Śrī Govindadeva's Itinerary from Vṛndāvana to Jayapura c. 1534–1727," ibid., pp. 160–83.

3. There is a good description of Jaipur in Alistair Shearer, *The Traveler's Guide to Northern India: A Guide to the Sacred Places of Northern India* (New York: Alfred A. Knopf, 1989), pp. 185–212.

4. See Monika Horstmann, "Govindadeva and His Custodians from 1643 through the Time of Jaya Siṃa II (1700–1743)," in Case, ed., *Govindadeva: A Dialogue in Stone,* pp. 185–93; Frederic Salmon Growse, *Mathurá: A District Memoir,* 3d ed. (Allahabad: North-Western Provinces and Oudh Government Press, 1883); and Margaret H. Case, "Growse in Context," *Journal of Vaiṣṇava Studies* 3.1 (Winter 1994): 141–52.

5. Conversation with Shrivatsa Goswami, June 1997.

6. I was privileged to be on the platform several times, to watch and take photographs.

7. See the discussion of this work and the translation of the first portion of it in Neal Delmonico, "How to Partake in the Love of Kṛṣṇa," in *Religions of India in Practice,* edited by Donald S. Lopez Jr. (Princeton: Princeton University Press, 1995), pp. 244–62.

8. The *Gauraṅga aṣṭayāma* by Candragopāla is a sixteenth-century text in Braj Bhāṣa that applies the concept of the līlās during the eight watches of the day to the life of Caitanya. See A.W. Entwistle, *Braj: Centre of Krishna Pilgrimage* (Groningen: Egbert Forsten, 1987), p. 55.

9. Conversation with Shrivatsa Goswami, June 1997.

10. A copy of the script for each of the aṣṭayāma līlās is in the archives of Sri Caitanya Prema Samsthana. I am grateful to Shrivatsa Goswami for making them available, and to Swapna Sharma and Brajbhushan Chaturvedi for helping me translate them. I did not see the performances of the 1989 lilā; the video recordings of them were made available to me, however.

Chapter 7

1. In 1989 and1992, this was Svāmi Śrīrāma Śarma; in 1995, it was Svāmi Fatehkṛṣṇa.

2. The theme of the theater of memory was developed by Barbara Stoler Miller in *The Theater of Memory: The Plays of Kālidāsa* (New York: Columbia University Press, 1984).

3. See Daniel H. H. Ingalls, "General Introduction," *Sanskrit Poetry from Vidyākara's "Treasury"* (Cambridge: Belknap Press of Harvard University Press, 1965), esp. pp. 11–16.

4. See, for example, the Introduction by Tridaṇḍī Svāmā Bhakti Hṛdaya Bon Mahārāj to his translation of the *Bhakti-Rasāmṛta-Sindhuḥ* of Śrī Rūpa Gosvāmī (Vrindaban: Institute of Oriental Philosophy, 1965), vol. 1.

Chapter 8

1. See the discussion and translation of the rāsalīlā on this theme in *At Play with Krishna: Pilgrimage Dramas from Brindavan* by John Stratton Hawley in association with Shrivatsa Goswami (Princeton: Princeton University Press, 1981), pp. 106–54.

2. The classic account of Holī celebration in a village is McKim Marriott, "The Feast of Love," in *Krishna: Myths, Rites, and Attitudes,* edited by Milton Singer (Chicago: University of Chicago Press, 1968), pp. 200–12.

3. He is recognized as such by the *Bhāgavata Purāṇa;* see Alain Daniélou, *Hindu Polytheism,* Bollingen Series 73 (New York: Pantheon, 1964), p. 165.

4. For the Rāmalīlās of Varanasi, see Philip Lutgendorf, *The Life of a Text: Performing the Rāmcaritmānas of Tulsīdās* (Berkeley and Los Angeles: University of California Press, 1991).

5. For a full description of sāñjī, see Asima Krishnadasa, *Evening Blossoms* (New Delhi: Indira Gandhi National Centre for the Arts, 1995).

6. The eighth līlā in 1992 was cut short by Mahārāj jī because a serious error was made in the production; the script was not preserved.

7. Mahārāj jī created the script for this līlā from folk tradition; the story is not part of the normal repertoire, as are the other līlās.

INDEX